Supernatural Ministry

Unleashing the Gifts Within You

Dr. James B. Richards

Impact International Publications
3300 N. Broad Place SW
Huntsville, AL 35805
(256)536-9402

*Not affiliated with Impact Publishers, Inc.
San Luis Obispo, California*

Impact International Publications
3300 N. Broad Place SW
Huntsville, AL 35805
(256)536-9402
Fax: (256)536-4530
e:mail: impact4god@aol.com
website: impactministries.com

Printed in the United States of America

Cover design by:
Millennium Graphics, Marietta, Georgia

Portrait of Dr. Richards by:
Terry Wowchuk, Winnipeg, Manitoba, Canada

Other Books by Dr. Richards:

Taking the Limits Off God
The Gospel of Peace
The Prayer Organizer
Grace: The Power to Change
Leadership That Builds People, Volume I:
Developing the Heart of a Leader
Leadership That Builds People, Volume II:
Developing Leaders Around You
My Church, My Family:
How to Have a Healthy Relationship
with the Church
Escape from Codependent Christianity
Satan Unmasked
Foundations of Faith Workbook
Relevant Ministry Workbook

Information also available about:

Impact International School of Ministry
Resident Program
Correspondence Program
External Degree Program
Tape & Book Catalog (free)

*To receive any of the above,
call or write today:*

Impact Ministries
3300 N. Broad Place SW
Huntsville, AL 35805
(256)536-9402 • Fax: (256)536-4530
E-mail: impact4god@aol.com
website: impactministries.com

Impact International School of Ministry

Impact International School of Ministry is raising up leaders who are able to meet the needs of this generation. The twentieth-century church is out of touch with the real needs of society. We have become a sub-culture that speaks a language no one understands. Our methods are outdated and ineffective. We are answering the questions that no one is asking, while ignoring and minimizing the ones that are being asked.

We have become like the religious community of Jesus' day. We cling to our tradition and make the Word of God of no effect. More than once I have looked at ultra-religious people and applied this verse to them. But, the truth is, any method I cling to that is no longer effective has become my tradition.

Tradition comes from things that were good; things that worked at one time. The church is like the children of Israel who didn't want to worship in the temple because they still clung to the tabernacle. That was good, but its time had past. God's life, presence and power was no longer there, it was time to move on.

Several major sources tell us that the majority of church growth in America is actually Christians going from one church to another. We are not really growing. The church has become a marketing agency that competes for those who know Jesus while abandoning those who do not know Him.

Impact International School of Ministry will

prepare you to reach this generation. Our commitment to the Word of God is absolute. Our commitment to methodology is as varied as the needs that exist. We are in touch with the world and we are on the cutting edge of what works.

If you are more interested in reaching the world than following the crowd, this may be the training program for you. Impact International School of Ministry has a resident program and an external program through which degrees can be earned. Call today for information:

Impact International School of Ministry
3300 N. Broad Place SW
Huntsville, AL 35805
(256)536-9402 ● (256)536-9876
Fax: (256)536-4530
E-Mail: impact4god@aol.com
website: impactministries.com

CONTENTS

1

A Living Organism

It seems that the present model of the effective church is somewhat different than what God envisioned in His heart and described in His Word. We tend to define the church in organizational concepts, which places an emphasis on structure instead of function.

The church should, however, be understood as a living organism that is going through continuous transformation. It is described in the Bible as a body, i.e., a living, growing organism that functions from the healthy synergism of every part. As a body, it is not only growing in size, but there is continuous transformation of each and every cell. It is a body that only maintains health and strength as every part does its job effectively.

In this body, there are no non-essential parts. There are no individual parts, which could be disposed of, without affecting the whole in some way. Like modern medicine, the modern clergyman looks at various parts and deems them insignificant and surgically removes them at the first sign of difficulty.

Individual members being denied the proper place of ministry and service has had much the same affect on the body of Christ as it would have on the human body. If there is not a continuous exchange of essential, life-giving nutrients, there is stagnant waste that leads to disease. The church, as a body, is daily becoming more crippled because individual members are not allowed to function in their place of ministry. The weakness of these members produces excess work for others parts of the body, which is a source of deterioration and disease.

While this book serves as a handbook to personal ministry, it is also a prescription for rebuilding a healthy church. It is a call for every Christian, "clergy or laity" to rethink the concepts of Christianity, discipleship and church. It is a call to personal ministry and personal development. Without one, the other is limited, if not impossible.

In order for the church to function as a living organism, we must accept the only job description given to the "clergy". It is found in Ephesians 4:11 and following. *"And he gave some, apostles; and some, prophets; and some, evangelists; and some, pastors and teachers; For the perfecting of the saints, for the work of the ministry, for the edifying of the body of Christ."*

It is the departure from this job description in the pursuit of personal fulfillment and self-exaltation that has corrupted and crippled the church. It is not the job of the clergy to rule over anyone.[1] Jesus refused the original apostles the right to rule over or exercise authority over one another.[2] Instead we are to serve

---

[1] *"Leadership That Builds People, Volume I,"* James B. Richards, Impact International Publications, Huntsville, Alabama

[2] Mark 10: 42-45

one another. The mark of being a leader in Christianity is not how you rule; it is how you serve.

We are to serve in a very specific way. We are to be motivated by love, governed by the irrefutable principles of the Word of God and empowered by the Spirit of Grace for the pursuit of a specific purpose. That purpose is found in verse 12 of Ephesians 4, *"For the perfecting of the saints, for the work of the ministry, for the edifying of the body of Christ."* There it is - the job description of the clergy.[3]

It is our job to perfect the saints. Unfortunately we have defined that as, *"to make them perfect."* So we have taken on Jesus' role, while praying for Him to do our job. "We'll get them right. God, You make them work." It is not our job to make people perfect. Jesus made every person perfect, holy, righteous and sanctified before God, when they participated in the new birth.

One familiar aspect of perfecting the saints is to *"equip them for works of service."* While this is certainly a valid aspect of the true meaning of the phrase, *"perfecting the saints,"* it is still a partial concept that gets the "cart before the horse." It is not simply about getting them to do the work.

Hidden within this phrase, *"equip the saints"* is an all-important concept. In Matthew 4:21, it tells of Jesus finding James and John. *"And going on from thence, he saw other two brethren, James the son of Zebedee, and John his brother, in a ship with Zebedee their father, mending their nets; and he called them."*

---

[3] While I personally detest the term "clergy," I use it simply for clarification. The concept of clergy and laity will be discussed in another chapter.

In the phrase *"mending their nets,"* the word "mending" is the same root word used in Ephesians 4:12. In Ephesians, it is translated as "perfecting."

The fishing nets were tools of the trade. These nets were cast out into the sea, and they were used to draw in the catch of new fish. However, as valuable as these nets were, they would be frustrating and of no value if they were not properly mended. We have grasped the concept of equipping God's people for works of service. We have totally failed, however, to mend them first.

In a living organism, every part has to do its job for the body to be healthy. We must realize, however, that people do not come to the church healthy. They come broken and torn. If they are thrown into the "work for God" mode before a degree of wholeness is reached, they will destroy themselves and others.

I see our job description as mending, making the believers whole, equipping them for works of service, and then launching them into a place of productivity. I cannot actually make a person whole. A person can only be made whole through the love of God. I facilitate that process of wholeness by teaching and modeling the love of God.

I want them to serve, not as a servant, but as a son. A person is not ready to serve until they have the revelation of sonship. Galatians 4:4-6. *"But when the fulness of the time was come, God sent forth his Son, made of a woman, made under the law, To redeem them that were under the law, that we might receive the adoption of sons. And because ye are sons, God hath sent forth the Spirit of his Son into your hearts, crying, Abba, Father."*

A servant serves out of fear; a son serves out of ownership. A servant is demeaned by his servitude; a son establishes dignity and worth by his servitude. A servant serves out of insecurity; a son serves out of complete security. A servant is faithful when he is seen; a son is forever faithful. To force a person to serve without some degree of wholeness causes much pain and suffering.

There is a paradox in this seemingly simple scenario. There is an aspect of personal growth that can only come by serving. It is here that we part into an either/or, dichotomous line of thinking. Either I focus on serving or I focus on personal growth. When I was first saved, I attended a denominational church for a short period of time. Before I was even sure who God was, I was being recruited to serve. Fortunately, I recognized that I was not ready to teach a Sunday School class. I knew I needed personal growth. There were areas where I served, and 1 am thankful for those opportunities.

Then I attended a charismatic church. They went to the other extreme. Everyone was so caught up in learning that they never felt mature enough to do anything. There was always a feeling that there was something else we needed to qualify us for service.

One group destroyed people launching them into areas of ministry prematurely, while the other pushed people into apathy by creating a sense of un-worthiness. While they both criticized the other, the end result was the same.

Every person should be involved in personal ministry, but only in an area where they are confident and developed. Stepping into personal ministry should be the outgrowth of each stage of personal growth. Wholeness should be expressed, in part, by accepting personal responsibility.

As we function at our present level of wholeness, we are prepared for future stages of growth and development. It is often this lack of personal service that causes us to get stuck in certain areas. It is certainly a major source of introspection and exaggerated self-interest.

Failure to accept our responsibility as personal ministers of the Gospel causes us to lose the sense of freshness and excitement we once had in the Lord. At this point, we either begin to pour out what we have, or we turn to synthetic stimulation like over sensationalism and mysticism. Others simply lose interest in the things of God.

As each member of the body of Christ functions at their level of personal wholeness, we become that living organism that is ever-serving, ever-growing and ever-changing. We change personally and individually, and we change as a body. We have that continuous exchange of life that can only come as we empty ourselves of that which we have in order to make room for fresh newness from the Spirit of God.

2

Unleashing the Power

You are filled with the power of God. All the power that God used to create the universe, the power that flowed through Jesus to heal the sick, raise the dead and work every miracle is resident inside you. The power is in you because the person of power is in you. The same Spirit that empowered Jesus is in you to empower you for works of service.

John 3:34 says, *"For he whom God hath sent speaketh the words of God: for God giveth not the Spirit by measure unto him."* The words "unto him" are not in the original text. We live in the day when the Holy Spirit is freely poured upon all men. The Spirit of God is not given to us in measure.

In the Old Testament, the Spirit of God did not inhabit the believer. He occasionally anointed the believer, but He never inhabited the believer. He was not holy, the Spirit of God could not live in him. We have been made righteous, clean and holy. We are a suitable dwelling wherein the Spirit of God may dwell.

To anoint means to "rub on." Because they only received an anointing, they never experienced the full measure of the Spirit. Jesus is the author and finisher of our faith. We look to Him to understand how a Son of God should function. He was the first. He showed the way. Jesus, not the Old Testament believer, is our model.

As a Son of God without sin, He demonstrated our relationship with the Holy Spirit. We are sons of God without sin. We are not looking for God to send us an anointing in the future when we obtain a better degree of righteousness by our works. Jesus made us as righteous as we can be. The Spirit of God came personally to dwell in us at the moment of our new birth. We do not have a measure of the Spirit. We have Him without measure.

Because the Holy Spirit is in you, all of His gifts are in you. Even if you do not believe in them, they are in you waiting to be used. The phrase "gifts of the Spirit" tends to be misleading. They are gifts only in the sense that they are freely given. However, the concept of gifts has lent itself to teaching that says that some have been given gifts that others have not. If you have been given a gift it is yours to do with as you wish.

The word "gift" has as its root the Greek word "charis." This word is the root word for "grace." Actually, healing, miracles, tongues, prophecy and all the other gifts of the Sprit are not gifts that are packaged and given to us; they are a work of grace. The word grace literally means power, ability or capacity. We do not have the power to heal, but the Spirit of God does. We do not have the ability to speak the mind of God, but His Spirit does.

We are vessels, in whom the Spirit of God dwells, with all the ability of God. As we yield to Him, He will allow that "ability" to flow out of us to express

God's love and power. So, why doesn't this happen more freely? We restrict the Spirit of God through our beliefs and personal limitations. We have been isolated from personal ministry by a clergy/laity paradigm that has robbed the church of power and effectiveness.

In the early church everyone ministered. Yes, there were different offices, but offices were about function, not position. God worked through believers, not offices. As time went by and the church slowly departed from its Biblical agenda, it became more political and social. Spiritual life gave way to organizational control.

Soon, there was a separation of the clergy and laity. The clergy presented itself as somehow closer to God; as possessing some special power that was kept from the lowly "laymen." Eventually, the clergy became the ones who ministered and the laity became the ones who served the clergy.

To a degree, that concept was modified with the reformation. In reality, however, the separation of clergy and laity continues just as strong as ever. It has simply changed its name and resurfaced in a new disguise.

Today you do not hear the word's clergy and laity used much. But you do hear a lot of talk about the "anointing." The anointing is presented as something that comes and goes based on any number of criteria. In the end, it is all the same. The guy standing on the platform has some aspect of "anointing" that you do not have. Of course, he earned this by adding something to the finished work of Jesus. He is somehow more deserving than you, so he has something of God that you do not have.

This anti-New Testament concept of anointing paralyzes the believer from a place of service. He does not know if he is anointed. He does not want to fail or do something to make God unhappy, so he seeks God and the "special preacher" for the anointing. Usually, the "anointed preacher" has the ability to lay hands on you and give you this anointing. At the end of the day, you are looking to a man to give you what Jesus has in fact already given you.

The Bible says, "you are anointed." 2 Corinthians 1:21 says, *"Now it is God who makes both us and you stand firm in Christ. He anointed us."* NIV. The great apostle, Paul, never claimed to have a different or better anointing, he only claimed to have a different responsibility.

We all have the same anointing. It was the one we received when we received Jesus. *"But the anointing which ye have received of him abideth in you, and ye need not that any man teach you: but as the same anointing teacheth you of all things, and is truth, and is no lie, and even as it hath taught you, ye shall abide in him."* 1 John 2:27. The early Gnostics tried to convince the believers that there were levels of anointing. John refuted this teaching in this verse.

He was not saying that no one needed teaching. God put teachers in the church. He was saying that we do not need special teachers to give us something from God. God gave us everything in Jesus. The Gnostics first created the sense of need in the people, then they offered to meet the need.[1] This is the very tactic that the serpent used in the garden, and this is the very

---

[1] *"Escape From Codependent Christianity,"* James B. Richards, Impact International Publications, Huntsville, Alabama

tactic that any controller uses today. First, he creates the sense of need, which can only be done by undermining trust in the finished work of Jesus. Then, he offers to meet that need.

The apostle John went on to let them know that he was not writing to them because he had something to add to them. 1 John 2:20-21 in the NIV says, *"But you have an anointing from the Holy One, and all of you know the truth. I do not write to you because you do not know the truth, but because you do know it and because no lie comes from the truth."* He wanted to affirm what they had in God. He was not offering to give them something that they did not have.

The only anointing emphasized in the New Testament is the "Anointed One." Jesus has the anointing. We are in Him. Therefore, we have the same anointing. If we did not receive it through His finished work, there is no one who can get it for us.

Our problem is not a lack of anointing. Our problem is a lack of confidence in the anointing. We fail to believe that God is in us, *"To will and to do His good pleasure."* We have accepted the religious myths that separate us from our place of service.

The clergy is seldom equipped to reach the person you see at work everyday. Most of the needs of mankind need to be met at home and at the workplace, not at the altar. We, the clergy, are to equip, mend and make you whole, so you can do the work of the ministry.

Because you and the millions of other believers around the world have been isolated from ministry, the church is impotent and failing to touch the world Jesus died to save. The need today is not for more anointed preachers.   The need is for more believers who will walk in the anointing Jesus gave.

As you trust God to flow through you, you will unleash this great power that abides in you. You will find a place of productive personal ministry that will change the world in which you live.

3

God's Secret Weapon

There is nothing as powerful as a secret weapon. It is the tool that works with the least amount of resistance, because it is not recognized as a threat. God's secret weapon is the believer. It is the believer that can quietly infiltrate the refuge of daily life and rescue those who have been taken captive by our enemy.

Many times when meeting someone new, I will not tell them that I am a minister. Because I have several other business interests, I usually identify myself with one of my businesses. The difference in the way people relate to me is amazing when they do not know that I am a preacher. I often infiltrate their defenses and lead them to Jesus before they ever know much about me.

You are God's secret weapon. You are like a "mole" planted in society, and it is time for you to become active. It is time for you to unleash this awesome power of God within you.

The average man and woman has always been the main vehicle for expansive ministry. It is rarely the professional preacher who really reaches the world. It was this way in the book of Acts. It was not the apostles who won the world, but the laymen, the believers who rubbed shoulders with the real world.

Jesus told the apostles to take the Gospel to Jerusalem, Judea, Samaria and to the uttermost parts of the earth. It was not the apostles who initiated this, it was the laymen. The apostles did preach the Word to the Jews at Jerusalem. Afterwards, they seemed to settle down and try to make Christianity a denomination of Judaism.

When persecution broke out against the church at Jerusalem, the believers were scattered and the apostles stayed in Jerusalem. As the believers scattered, they preached the Word. *"Therefore they that were scattered abroad went everywhere preaching the word."* Acts 8:4.

It was Phillip, the deacon, who preached the Word and worked miracles at Samaria. Until then, the apostles let their racial prejudice prevent them from ministering to the Samaritans. As always, it was the laymen who lived with the real people that scaled the walls of social prejudice. The apostles only came to establish them after they received the Word.

After leaving Samaria, Phillip met the Ethiopian Eunuch. Phillip ministered to the African and was then supernaturally caught away. This Ethiopian carried the Word of God to the Queen of Ethiopia, thus, we had the birth of Christianity in Africa. When the apostles later arrived, there was already a church.

When Paul was converted in Acts 9, it was not an apostle who received the vision and the commission to minister to him. It was a layman, by the name of Ananias. The apostles didn't trust Paul. It was another layman, Barnabas, who accepted and discipled Paul.

Then in Acts chapter 10, we have the centurion in Ceaesarea praying and seeking God. God gave him a vision about where to find the apostle Peter. Peter would have never gone to minister to this man because he considered him unclean. God visited Peter with a vision, and he reluctantly went with the Gentiles and proclaimed the Word of God to them. While preaching to them, the Spirit of God fell on the Gentiles. This caused such a stir in Jerusalem that a social counsel was called to sort out how they would theologically justify this event. Once again the apostles would never have gone to the Gentiles. They could hardly cope with it, when God Himself initiated it. A lost Gentile was the obedient layman who was responsible for this revival.

In Acts 11, the apostles sent Barnabas to Antioch because there was a church that had sprung up there. Once again, it was a church that was established independently of the apostles at Jerusalem. It was this very church that eventually became the center of all world evangelism. It was this church that fulfilled the commission that the apostles were unwilling to fulfill.

Acts 19: 10 says, *"And this continued by the space of two years; so that all they which dwelt in Asia heard the word of the Lord Jesus, both Jews and Greeks."* We read this verse, and in our mind, we see Paul blazing the missionary trail to win the entire world to Jesus. Actually, the previous verse makes this a little clearer, *"He... separated the disciples, disputing daily in the school of one Tyranus."* Paul taught daily in the school of Tyranus. It was those who heard that went forth and spread the Good News that they were hearing.

We have a role crisis in the church. We expect the clergy to do our job. In so doing, their job is totally neglected. In the end, the world suffers, Christians do not grow, and the Kingdom of God does not advance.

It is the job of the five-fold ministry to equip and make you whole through the love of God. It is your role to minister to the world with whom you have daily contact. As long as there is a role reversal, there will be confusion and weakness in the church.

Step into your God-given place as a son. From that position of son-ship, assume the responsibility as a son. You will experience explosive personal growth and the needs of many will be met through Christ in you.

4

Ministry and Priorities

As the body of Christ in the earth, it is essential that we function in accordance with the head. With Christ as the head, we, the church, must follow Him. We must function in accordance with His will. A body that cannot function in accordance with the head (mind) is limited, non-effective and even spastic.

Because the church has not had the same priorities as the head, we have been unable to function properly in this world. We say that we want to do the works of the Lord Jesus, yet we have completely different priorities and objectives. This is clearly demonstrated by the way we spend our time, money and energy. Regardless of our words, our priorities manifest in our actions.

Jesus plainly stated and pursued His objectives. *"For the Son of man is come to seek and to save that which was lost."* Luke 19:10. Jesus' entire ministry was done with the clear-cut priority of setting people free. Although He was the embodiment of the five-fold ministry, He never let anything supersede His call to reach the lost and set the captives free. His office did not alleviate Him from the responsibility to minister. Instead, His office facilitated His purpose.

"For this purpose the Son of God was manifested, that He might destroy the works of the devil." 1 John 3:8. Jesus ministered to every need of mankind. He tore down every stronghold in a person's life, yet He never got side tracked into "specialized ministry." He knew the reason for tearing down strongholds was to bring a person into an abundant, loving relationship with the Father. Knowing God, the Father through the Lord Jesus Christ is salvation, freedom and joy.

Jesus used the gifts of the Holy Spirit as tools to break the strongholds. The gifts never became the central theme; they were, however, vehicles to arrive at the desired destination.

Unlike the religious leaders of His day (and ours), He did not depend on mere arguments and theological debates to persuade people. Winning an argument never set anyone free from anything, but the gifts of the Holy Spirit demonstrate the love and goodness of God in a way people can personally experience. Jesus was ever dependent on the Holy Spirit to empower Him to meet the needs of the people. Acts 10:38 says it this way, *"How God anointed Jesus of Nazareth with the Holy Ghost and with power: who went about doing good, and healing all that were oppressed of the devil; for God was with him."*

Effective evangelism can only be done when we, like Jesus, tear down every bondage, every stronghold, every work of the devil, and allow men and women to experience the power of God. Paul realized this could not be done through persuasiveness and arguments. He knew it would take the power of God demonstrated to make men trust in God. *"And my speech and my preaching was not with enticing words of man's wisdom, but in demonstration of the Spirit and of power: That your faith should not stand in the wisdom of men, but in the power of God.*" 1 Corinthians 2:4-5.

Jesus assured us that the power to do the works He did was not limited to His early disciples, but it was for all who believed. "*Verily, verily, I say unto you, He that believeth on me, the works that I do shall he do also; and greater works than these shall he do; because I go unto my Father.*" John 14: 12.

Jesus perpetuated His priority as He trained the disciples. While the disciples had the opportunity to hear all of Jesus' great sermons, they were also eyewitnesses to His ministry. Jesus trained them in such a way that their level of truth was paralleled by the opportunity to put it into practice.

During His life there were arguments about denominationalism. "*And John answered him, saying, Master, we saw one casting out devils in thy name, and he followeth not us: and we forbade him, because he followeth not us.*" Mark 9:38. Later there were power struggles. They said unto him, "*Grant unto us that we may sit, one on thy right hand, and the other on thy left hand, in thy glory.*" Mark 10:37.

Despite all this practical training, the disciples, like the church of today, were easily moved from the God-given priority. In the first chapter of Acts, Jesus was giving His last personal address to the disciples. It is obvious that these would be crucial words for the future of the church.

As He began to explain the baptism in the Holy Spirit, the disciples interrupted His teaching to ask, "Is this when you will restore the kingdom to Israel?"

(Acts 1:6). Verse seven is a mild rebuke. "*And he said unto them, It is not for you to know the times or the seasons, which the Father hath put in his own power.*" Acts 1:7. They had their priorities wrong; they wanted the end to come. They wanted to be delivered from this world; they wanted to break the bondage of Rome off their necks. Jesus, on the other hand, wanted them to be powerful witnesses who would minister to the entire world.

Maintaining Biblical priority has always been a great difficulty for the church. Every denomination, every organization and every sect of Christianity has its own personal substitutes. Many times these substitutes are the product of ignorance, but too often they are a product of choice. We **think** we know what it will take to build strong churches. Yet, apart from the church fulfilling its role in the earth, it will never see real growth that reaches the numbers and the hearts.

When Jesus explained the purpose of the baptism in the Holy Spirit, He emphasized two points: what you could BE and what you could DO because the Holy Spirit is upon you. Because of what you will BE, you will DO witnessing. Witnessing should always be the product of what you ARE, more than what you DO. By the power of the Holy Spirit, witnessing can be effective, fruitful and joyful. Otherwise, it becomes a means of earning things from God.

In Luke 4:18, Jesus explained why the Holy Spirit was upon Him. All of these reasons were for ministry. The Holy Spirit comes IN you to work in your life and character. However, He comes UPON you for the purpose of ministry. The Bible commands us not to grieve the Holy Spirit. When we refuse to allow Him to fulfill His ultimate purpose for being UPON us, He is grieved.

Only by adjusting our priorities will we find fulfillment and purpose in our walk with the Lord. It is somewhat frightening to consider answering the call to be a witness, but it starts with a decision. Remember, He did not say you would DO witnessing; He said you would BE a witness. He will do a work in you to make witnessing as natural as breathing.

Before proceeding in this book you may want to pray this prayer:

> *"Father, forgive me for not being a witness. Forgive me for getting side tracked. Help me to establish right priorities. I admit my fears, weaknesses, and unwillingness in this area of my life. Change my heart so that I will be a witness to those around me. Give me compassion for others. Let your love flow out of me. Amen."*

This book is not designed to get you to "DO WITNESSING." Its purpose is to show you some divine truth with which God can work in your heart. **Doing** the right thing is always contingent on **being** the right thing. As you read these pages, faith and grace will begin to rise in your heart. God will prepare you for an exciting life of supernatural ministry. You, like Jesus, can live a life that is an open channel for the gifts of the Holy Spirit to flow through you and touch others.

As you commit to the divine priorities of the Lord Jesus, new meaning, purpose and power will come into your life.

5

Evangelism and Church History

When Jesus departed from planet Earth, He gave what has come to be known as the Great Commission. *"Go ye therefore, and teach all nations, baptizing them in the name of the Father and the Son, and the Holy Spirit."* Matthew 28:19. This is the only commission given to the church. This is not one of the reasons we are here; it is the **only** reason we are here. This is our top priority. When our priorities do not place ministry as our number one function, our priorities are wrong.

The early church was consumed with this commission. The words of Jesus were still ringing in their ears, *"And this Gospel of the kingdom shall be preached in all the world for a witness unto all nations; and then shall the end come."* Matthew 24: 14. They had seen and experienced what Jesus would do on earth. They wanted Him to return. They wanted the Kingdom to be established. They knew they had the responsibility of proclaiming this gospel around the world so Jesus could return.

The commitment to God's priorities produced excitement, activity and power. As they were about the Father's business, they saw the healings, miracles and signs. Yet it was not long until purpose gave way to reason. Evangelism became "bogged down" in theological debate, religious performance and ritual.

All serious evangelism had stopped by 90-100 AD. In the Book of Revelation, the church was being rebuked for its self-centered, noncommittal state of being (Rev. 2-3). From all indications, evangelism in Jerusalem had stopped just a few short years after Jesus ascended.

The apostles settled down into a comfortable, religious life. It seems they would have settled the church in as a sect (denomination) of Judaism, right along with Pharisees and Sadducees, if it had not been for the persecution. *"And Saul was consenting unto his (Stephen's) death. And at that time there was a great persecution against the church which was at Jerusalem; and they were all scattered abroad throughout the regions of Judaea and Samaria, except the apostles."* Acts 8:1. At the time of the persecution, the church scattered; as they went, they proclaimed the gospel. The center for all Christian activity shifted from Jerusalem to Antioch. We see the beginning of the ministry of the apostle Paul in Acts 13.

By 300 A.D. the church had become dead, social and powerless. The absence of real evangelism brought about the greatest corruption of government and mankind the world had ever seen. It was not until the time of the Reformation that the church returned to Biblical evangelism. Once again, she became a spiritual force that changed nations by changing hearts.

History bears out that the church has always failed as a political force. In our nation, we have the opportunity and obligation to be politically involved individuals. The reality is this: If the church does not bring change through relevant ministry, it will have no more influence than another political party. Righteousness cannot be legislated; it must come through the hearts of men who make Jesus Lord and receive righteousness of heart.

On a trip to China, I heard a historical review of that nation. The political condition of the country went hand-in-hand with the degree of evangelization. The lecturer paralleled the vulnerability of China to the degree of evangelism and ministry that was being done. The condition of the people determined their ability to be swayed into captivity by foreign governments.

The strength of any nation is determined by the righteousness of the people, not the fairness of their constitution. *"Righteousness exalteth a nation: but sin is a reproach to any people."* Proverbs 14:34. Righteousness only comes when people believe and commit to the Lordship of Jesus. *"For with the heart man believeth unto righteousness; and with the mouth confession is made unto salvation."* Romans 10:10.

Most Christians would love to blame the political condition on "super spiritual" reasons. They love to assume God is judging countries and bringing about their fall. The truth of the matter is this: If we do not win the lost and develop disciples, our country will become corrupt and fall through the theft, murder, deceit and corruption that we sow. God does not have to overthrow a corrupt nation; it rots of its own accord.

As the church moves away from God's priorities, it loses power and influence. It is then put in a position to create false spirituality. Gimmicks give way to life and power. Before long, the church is nothing more than a voice. God did not call us to be a voice; we are called to be a force. *"For the kingdom of God is not in word, but in power."* 1 Corinthians 4:20.

When the church returns to Biblical ministry, it will be free from the picket lines and the courtrooms. When political leaders are saved and developed into disciples, they will look to pastors, the Bible and the Holy Spirit for understanding.

In the early years of this nation, the Bible was the guiding principle in law making, education and morality. We still have the same laws and schools founded by those men. However, with immoral men interpreting the constitution and controlling education, that godly foundation is of no value.

When our judges, political leaders, and educators are won to Jesus, they will have no trouble interpreting our laws or educating our children.

The future of our nation will be determined by the church's willingness to win and disciple the lost. History is written in the hearts of the believers.

6

Living in the Vision

Evangelism is the best all-around investment of time and effort ever made by a church or individual. In a day when pastors are insecure about losing members, and churches accuse each other of "sheep stealing," peace could come by every church simply reaching into their own community through evangelism.

There is a cycle that churches or individuals often enter. I have seen it repeatedly over the past twenty-five years. I call it the cycle of death. All churches begin with, or at some time acquire, a vision. Maintaining that vision is essential for life. A vision produces energy, excitement and activity. Many individuals begin their walk with God with a strong vision of personal ministry.

The word "vision," as used in the original language is not speaking of a vision from God. It means "a clear mental picture." That vision should be a combination of scriptural priority and the personal call of God. Every pastor should have a clear-cut vision for his life and ministry. As he presents the scriptural priorities to the people, they develop the ability to see it in their hearts. Seeing that clear picture provides confidence, stability and purpose.

Purpose is the strongest motivation there is. When people see that God is using them, when they see their church has a direction and when that direction is consistent with the Biblical priorities, the Holy Spirit will empower that purpose. Because man is created in the likeness of God and God is love, we, like God, have a need to live beyond ourselves. Jesus said the way to have is to give, the way to rule is to serve, and the way to live is to die to self. Man has the God-given need to live for a cause beyond himself. This cause produces a strong sense of motivation.

The absence of a vision produces laziness, apathy and even sin. *"Where there is no vision, the people perish..."* Proverbs 29:18. The New International Version accurately translates "perish" as, "cast off restraints." When people have no deep sense of purpose, they first lose motivation, then they cast off restraints. A church with no clear-cut Biblical purpose that reaches beyond itself will be a breeding ground of gossip, division and every evil practice.

So the beginning of every church or ministry is a vision. That vision, if it is Biblical, will produce the passion and energy that brings about growth. For most churches, there is a greater percentage of growth the first year than the rest of its history. It should, however, be just the opposite.

Growth brings its own set of problems. Preachers are like doctors in that all of their patients are sick. The people they reach have problems; that is why they go to them. It is their job to help set them free. Matthew 28:19 tells us the two parts of the great commission: evangelize and teach (disciple). It seems that few ministries are capable of doing both. There-

fore, as growth comes, they feel forced into choosing
between quality and quantity.

It is at this point that most ministers go into the
management phase. In the management phase they lose
their vision. They do not give it all up at one time, but
the demands of the people slowly obscure that clear
mental picture. They become "bogged down" in the
details of management until necessity outweighs priority.

It is at this point that the ministers begin to
"cool down." They leave the realm of excitement and
joy, and enter the world of the "professional minister."
The "management ministry" has stolen more calls than
sin itself. With this loss of purpose, the minister will
cast off restraints. If he does not restore his vision, he
will become a pharisaical leader, fall into apathy or get
into sin.

In the management phase, leaders begin to do
for people what Jesus Himself did not do for them.
They take on the load of personal problems. Worse
than all that, they try to possess them. "Management"
usually translates into: "Now I have to find a way to
keep what I have." Much of what we do in the name of
ministry is a very subtle way to control. We want to
know all the details of a person's life so we can advise
them in such a way as to keep them in our church.

This is the ultimate breeding ground for strife.
At this point, we stop preaching the messages that drew
the crowds and helped the people. Now we begin
preaching the messages that will keep people in our
church and bring them under our control. This is when
we start preaching about "covering, submission, commitment and church loyalty." This is where preachers

become angry and use the pulpit as a "whipping post."

Since our goal has now become maintaining, we no longer have the power and joy like we did at the beginning. Growth slows to a near stop, and people begin to question leadership. "Why aren't we growing? Why isn't it like it used to be? What is wrong here?"

At this point, we enter into the justification stage. In this stage we justify why it is not like it used to be. We even create convenient doctrines to preserve our self-worth. We become so defensive that we cannot see the truth. During this time, we become unapproachable and condescending to the people.

Ministry is the epitome of free enterprise. When people leave, become dissatisfied or question leadership, we should examine ourselves. We should examine the direction and purpose of our ministry. It is rare that another pastor actually "steals church members," people leave because they want to. This should be an indicator of the quality and scope of ministry we offer.

The next stage is death. Death does not mean you close the doors. It does not mean you do not grow numerically. Death is when you no longer live for your vision, call and purpose. This is the present condition of most ministers and churches. All that is required for life to return is simple repentance. Return to your vision. If your vision was wrong then you must develop a Biblical vision. Pray it, preach it, teach it and live it.

You may lose some people by returning to a scriptural vision, but growth will return if you persist in a godly vision. Do not be so afraid of your people that you cannot get help, admit to being wrong and turn the ministry around. God can restore you to your first love so you will once again do your first works with peace, purpose and joy.

I have often had to admit that our church was not able to meet the needs of some people. Rather than condemn those people, these became valuable times of personal evaluation.

Sometimes, the loss of a member gave me the "reality call" that I needed to bring quality to a particular area of ministry. I often came to realize that I would probably never develop our ministry in the area of their need.

The essential point is, do not enter into justification. Justification propels you into the death phase.

7

The Investment of Evangelism

Evangelism is the best ministerial investment one can ever make. Besides the eternal benefits of souls brought into the Kingdom of God, besides the realization of the great commission, besides the gratification that comes from being in the center of God's will, it is the only sure way to fulfill the vision. Growth, which does not come through evangelism and outreach, does not normally promote peace. It is only an exchange of problems. We simply inherit the problems generated in the last church our new members attended. These are usually people who need deliverance from wrong attitudes and strange doctrines. They do not come into your church with the excitement, warmth and enthusiasm that attracts others to your church. It is usually just the opposite; they bring attitudes and problems that repel others.

If a person comes into your church for positive reasons, it can work. If the Lord speaks to his heart, if he is coming to serve, or possibly you are able to meet certain needs, it may work out. But when a person comes because of what he is against in his last church, it seldom works.

Evangelism in itself creates healthy growth, but there is a double benefit of growth. Because of the excitement of forgiveness and peace, a new believer will be a channel to an entirely new set of unreached people. Through the new convert, you can touch lives which you would have never before had access or opportunity to touch. Reaching the churched people will only give you access to people who are already attending other churches.

Personal evangelism, which is the most effective, is a tremendous financial investment. For the cost of tracts and a few Bibles, you can reach people, bring them into your church and increase church finances. All of our new converts are more consistent at tithing and giving than the ones who have "made the circuit."

The excitement of a new believer is contagious. They infect the congregation with joy. They bring in an enthusiasm that stirs the entire church. Many great revivals in the local church have started by reaching one excited person. This is especially true among the teens and young adults. One excited young person is like a breath of fresh air that will blow in more excitement and new converts than the efforts of an entire church. And be assured that enthusiasm reaches far more people than doctrine.

Several years ago we had a real revival among our young people. Every time I came to church there would be full rows of people brought to church by one or two of our young people. Young people tend to vocalize their excitement more than older people; therefore, they often reach more people. When I would give an altar call, our young people would take the visitors by the hand and bring them to the altar. Many of them are still walking with the Lord today.

The love that God has is a love that gives. This love is most clearly demonstrated when it is given to those who are unlovable. Evangelism promotes this kind of love. A church that is reaching out, is a church that is patient and kind. It recognizes faults as areas that need ministry. A church that is reaching out will not be "reaching in." A church that is giving love is usually experiencing love.

When people's attention is not on the harvest, they tend to look inward to try and solve everyone's problems. In an attempt to make everyone mature, faultfinding is passed off as "discernment." The church is then so failure oriented and full of discord, it cannot attract new people.

A church that is simply trying to be mature does not minister to faults; it criticizes them. When a church is not reaching out, it is reaching in through introspection, works righteousness and comparison. Because the love and life of God is not flowing out to others, criticism and strife set in.

Many churches use the excuse "We have to get things in order before we try to reach out." The truth is, order never comes to a church that is out of the "divine order" of scriptural priority. God has never called any church or ministry to exist without reaching the lost as a priority.

Evangelism and personal ministry is the place of discipling new converts. Jesus did not teach the apostles in a classroom; He took them to the people. They saw and participated in ministry. His technique of discipling produced world-changing Christians in three and a half years. Our techniques take a lifetime.

Because we want everyone to be perfect before we ever allow them to do anything for the Lord, we create a rejection mentality that says, "If I cannot do it perfect, I will just bury my talents in the ground." We make new converts become lazy, self-centered pew-warmers.

If we involve new believers in evangelism, follow-up and personal ministry, they will see that God can work through them. Then they become less dependent on leadership and learn to be an asset to the church, rather than a liability. Most pastors bemoan the lack of help that comes from the church members, yet the pastor is the first to deny them the right to serve and grow.

Christians who are not involved in ministry only have a theoretical understanding of the Word. So, every time they have a problem they call the pastor for help. Instead of becoming dependent on Jesus, they become dependent on the pastor. Instead of maturing, they become more self-centered. The end result is a church full of people who demand very much from the pastor and give very little of themselves.

On the other hand, Christians who share their faith become keenly aware that God can work through them. Seeing God meet needs in others makes them more confident that He can and will meet their personal needs. Philemon 6 says it this way in the NIV, "*I pray that you may be active in sharing your faith, so that you will have a full understanding of every good thing we have in Christ.*" I say it this way; "Proclamation brings revelation."

A proper approach to evangelism produces

strong, fruit-bearing Christians who are able to bear the burden of ministry and lighten the load of the pastor. It produces strong, stable Christians who have purpose, power and victory. Christians who are reaching out require very little encouragement and counsel. They grow as they go. They are encouraged by the joy of the Lord. They are too busy meeting the needs of others to be bogged down in self-centered, petty problems.

Personal evangelism becomes a great investment in the community. It is a tremendous investment in the church. Moreover, it is a powerful investment in our own personal development.

8

Ministry and Personal Growth

Churches that have a strong emphasis on discipleship usually abandon personal ministry. I have often heard the pastor say, "When we get the people established, we're going to begin to reach out." The problem is, however, the mystical place of "being established" is never found.

American methods of discipleship do not produce strong, stable Christians who are able to minister independently. In our desire to control, we have made people feel as if they cannot function without the pastor's express approval. The truth is, no one needs their pastor's approval to do anything Jesus told them to do.

In our attempt to keep people from failing, we have completely immobilized the church. While conducting a soul-winning meeting a few years ago, a lady visited from another church. She was completely shocked when we sent them out door-to-door, after only ninety minutes of instruction. She had been attending a soul winning class for nearly a year. She had memorized dozens of scriptures, read books and heard sermons, but had not witnessed to anyone.

That day, after ninety minutes of training, she went out with a group that led seventeen people to the Lord. She gained more spiritual stamina and excitement that day than all those weeks of training. As a matter of fact, all those weeks of training had begun to convince her that she was incapable of effective personal ministry.

There is something about the classroom instruction mentality that prohibits maturity, instead of stimulating it. The people, who get active in DOING the gospel, grow. The ones who study the gospel never seem to develop.

Our church has a strong emphasis on prayer. Because I have authored a publication called "*The Prayer Organizer*" all of our people know about prayer. Oftentimes we will reach a person who has been on drugs, lived an immoral life and a host of other problems. We will hand them a "*Prayer Organizer*" and tell them to start a prayer life. Even though they know very little about God, they will live in consistent victory. At the same time those who know about it, but do not do it are failing miserably.

In Philemon 6 Paul said this, "*I pray that you may be active in sharing your faith, so that you will have a full understanding of every good thing we have in Christ*" (NIV). Under the inspiration of the Holy Spirit, Paul prays for and explains one of the great values of personal ministry. It helps you have an understanding of THE GOOD THINGS YOU HAVE IN CHRIST.

There is a supernatural strength that comes from sharing your faith. A revelation emerges that comes no other way. You partake of the divine life you pour out. After moving into an old house and remodeling major potions of the plumbing, I saw something interesting. Whatever minerals are in the water that flowed through the pipe formed a residue on the inside of the pipe. The pipe was no longer the material it was originally made of, but it was now the material it had become by the water that flowed through it. Likewise, when we allow the Holy Spirit to flow through us, He leaves a "residue of life" in us. We partake of what we pour out.

One of the great benefits of preaching is the regaining of spiritual strength. Paul says it this way, *"Because we believe, we speak."* 2 Corinthians 4:13. He did not say, "Because I have it all working, I speak," He said, "because I believe, I speak." Believing the truth qualifies you to proclaim the truth.

The devil will always try to stop you from speaking. He will accuse you of being a hypocrite because you still have problems. He will say, "You are going to tell someone about Jesus with all of your problems? Look at you; you are a wreck. You cannot help anyone." A hypocrite is not someone who does not have it all worked out; a hypocrite is someone who tries to make others **think** he has it all worked out.

Many times I have come to the place where I felt like quitting, but I have never given into the temptation to stop speaking. While I was fighting for my life due to a kidney disorder, I continued to preach healing. Many times I would preach a strong healing message and give an effective altar call, only to lay across the bed afterwards to receive a life-sustaining injection. Condemnation would harass my mind, but I would not stop sharing my faith. The more I shared, the stronger I became. Because I would not throw away my confidence, healing soon became my reality.

When I have faced tremendous financial problems, I never stopped preaching about God's ability and willingness to provide. The devil harassed me, circumstances embarrassed me and staff members came against me, but I continued to speak. Never be intimidated into silence. Do not try to pretend you are something you are not. Do not be a phony, but do not disqualify yourself because you do not have it all working in your life.

As you share the life of God with others, even in the areas you are weak, an understanding will come into you by the Holy Spirit. You will have insight into the areas where you are weak. Paul said weakness was the perfect place to find God's grace. "*And he said unto me, My grace is sufficient for thee: for my strength is made perfect in weakness. Most gladly therefore will I rather glory in my infirmities, that the power of Christ may rest upon me.*" 2 Corinthians 12:9.

In the King James Version, Philemon 6 reads like this: "*That the communication of thy faith may become effectual by the acknowledging of every good thing which is in you in Christ Jesus.*" That word "effectual," according to Strong's, means operative or powerful. Many times the truth you know becomes operative only as you share it with others.

Truth becomes effectual, or operative, by the acknowledging of every good thing in you in Christ. That word "acknowledging" means "recognition, full discerning or understanding." The original word in the Greek comes from a word that means, "to know experientially." Sharing will often transport you from believing to experiential knowledge.

Many times I have shared a truth that I believed, but was not experiencing at that moment. As I would see others believe and receive, understanding would come into me about my situation. I do not know how many people got healed under my ministry while I was sick. I did not understand about healing at that time, but I did believe it. I actually learned from those who were receiving.

Ministering to others brings a maturity that comes no other way. Therefore, waiting to witness until maturity comes is a violation of scriptural procedure for growth. Maturity, after all, is not what you know; it is what you can walk in. An operative, powerful faith comes from a full understanding, which comes as you share your faith.

The believer who does not step into the realm of personal ministry will forever abide in the realm of information. The one who shares his faith will enter new realms of experiential knowledge and maturity.

9

The Creative Nature of the Believer

2 Corinthians 5:17 says, "*Therefore, if anyone is in Christ, he is a new creation; the old has gone the new has come.*" (NIV) Learning to adapt to our new nature is one of the joys and challenges of becoming a Christian. At the new birth, one is made alive unto God. His spirit is alive; he is God-conscious. Because our nature is changed, we can no longer conduct ourselves in the same manner as before. What we used to do without any pain is now contrary to our new nature.

This is the beginning of a lifetime of transformation into the likeness of Christ. For the convert who does not grasp this difference in himself and yield to it, the Christian walk will be unfulfilling at best. As people who desire to please God, let's look at Christ, the author and finisher of our faith, and realize that God intends to make us like Him. "*For whom he did foreknow, he also did predestinate to be conformed to the image of his Son, that he might be the firstborn among many brethren.*" Romans 8:29.

The only pattern for understanding the changes God will work in our life is Jesus Himself. God was so pleased with His Son that He determined to have an entire family that would be just like Him. Because we have looked at people as our pattern, we have tried to get God to make us like someone other than Jesus.

Years ago an "ex-hippie" friend of mine got saved. He was a longhaired rebel, like most of my friends. He was as anti-establishment as they came. When I got saved, I recommended to all my friends to change the way we dressed and wore our hair. But, this one brother went to the extreme. He went into a training program led by a particular denomination. When he came home, he looked like someone had cut him out with a preacher shaped cookie cutter.

He had the right kind of suit, wing-tipped shoes; hair parted slightly off to one side of the middle and combed straight back. I almost laughed when I saw him. This thought ran through my mind, "God will not know who to bless when you pray because He does not know who you are any more."

God does not need our imitation of anyone; He needs for us to be transformed into the likeness of Jesus.

This transformation is a process that works from the inside out. Inside we are righteous and holy. That which is in us is transforming our outer man.

While preaching in a meeting recently, I met another young preacher. Boy, was he a good preacher! If I had shut my eyes, I would have thought I was listening to R.W. Shambach. As we talked, I soon learned he was struggling financially. While he had a good ministry, it seemed there was nothing distinct about his ministry; he was just preaching. As I prayed for him, the Lord spoke to my heart and said, "Son, I do not need his imitation of R.W. Shambach. I have one Shambach, I do not need another. I need for him to be what I have called *him* to be in Jesus."

In Genesis 1:26-27, God said, *"Let us make man in our image, in our likeness,... So God created man in His own image, in the image of God He created them..."* Man was created to have the same character qualities as God. Moreover, at the new birth, he is predestined to be conformed to the likeness of Christ. The righteous nature received at the new birth permeates every aspect of our character as we yield to it.

Because we are made in the image of God and are being conformed to the likeness of Christ, there is an aspect of our nature that is easily overlooked. That is: We have a desire, a need, and a demand in us to create life. Every believer has a creative aspect built into his nature. Why? It is God's nature and God's character to give life. God is a life-giver. Everything God does produces life. Jesus said, *"...I have come that they may have life..."* John 10:10 NIV. Likewise, every believer has a built-in desire to give life.

Many have said that we are most like God in the creative sense because we have the ability to give birth to children. This is true to a certain degree. But after salvation we are most like God, in the creative sense, in that we have the commission to carry the Gospel of life. Because we know the Author of life, we are now commissioned to carry the Word of life to a world that is dead in sin (Ephesians 2: 1-5).

I believe with all my heart there is a part of our nature that will never be fulfilled or satisfied apart from giving life through the Gospel of Jesus Christ. There is a hunger that cannot be filled. There is a longing in the life of any believer who has not learned to satisfy this aspect of his new nature.

We, the church, are the body of Christ and He is the head. It is only natural then that the body is controlled by the thoughts of the head. Jesus, our head, has not changed (Hebrews 13:8). His mission on earth is the same, *"To seek and to save that which was lost."* Luke 10:10. We, as the body, can only demonstrate God's will if we move under the direction of the Head.

In John 5: 19, Jesus gave them this answer: *"I tell you the truth, the Son can do nothing by Himself; He can only do what He sees the Father doing, because whatever the Father does the Son also does."* Jesus was powerful and effective because He continually did what He saw the Father doing. We, as the church, can only be powerful and effective when we do what we see the Son doing. A simple study of the Gospels will reveal that Jesus spent His life spreading the Good News. Likewise, we, as His body on earth today, should have that one thing in first priority on our list of obedience.

The earmark of our modern society is a lack of direction and purpose. The two go hand-in-hand. Only when one has direction can they have purpose. Purpose provides motivation and hope. Only when there is purpose can there be achievement. Only when there is achievement can there be satisfaction and self-confidence. Unfortunately, this same malady has invaded the church, no clear-cut direction, therefore, no purpose, no satisfaction, and no motivation. When a believer has no purpose why should he read his Bible? Why should he tithe, why come to church, or do anything other than sit around and wait for Jesus' return. Even worse, what would stop him from falling into sin? If the individual believer or the local church is to be victorious and powerful, there must be a clearly defined purpose and a plan for bringing that purpose to fruition.

Because of this lack of clear-cut direction, many leaders have a hard time knowing where they are to lead the people. How frustrating it must be to be in a position of leadership and not really know exactly where it is you are supposed to lead the people.

In recent years, the body of Christ has experienced degrees of restoration through teaching. Many of the truths that had been seemingly lost for years have been restored, bringing the body back to a place of power and truth. But for what purpose have we regained this power and truth? Nothing less than making a real impact on the world for Jesus. Truth is not an end within itself. As a matter of fact, there is no greater frustration than to have amassed a great wealth of knowledge and to have no practical outlet.

The Scripture teaches that we must not merely hear the Word, we must do what it says. *"But be ye doers of the word, and not hearers only, deceiving your own selves. For if any be a hearer of the word, and not a doer, he is like unto a man beholding his natural face in a glass: For he beholdeth himself, and goeth his way, and straightway forgetteth what manner of man he was. But whoso looketh into the perfect law of liberty, and continueth therein, he being not a forgetful hearer, but a doer of the work, this man shall be blessed in his deed."* James 1:22-25. A leader, therefore, must be one who not only knows and proclaims the truth, but also one who is able to make that truth applicable to the main purpose of the Christian call. We, as leaders, then want to first lead people into a quality relationship with the Lord Jesus Christ.

Our second objective is to bring every believer into fulfillment of purpose. This is only done when one gratifies the creative nature he received at the new birth. Try as we may, apart from ministering to others, fulfillment will always be illusive.

When I was first saved, I would have cravings that I could not identify. I can remember thinking, "Am I hungry?" I would eat but not be satisfied. At times I would take a nap only to wake up and not be rested. I soon learned that I had a "spiritual appetite." Now that I was born again, I had spiritual needs that had to be fulfilled. My heart would crave prayer, the Word and fellowship with the Lord. Besides this, there was an intense desire to pour out life.

Ministry has never been something we have to do to please God. It has been something that satisfies our new nature. God's love for the world compels us to minister life to those who will hear. If a person ignores this long enough, hardness of heart will render him insensitive to the Lord.

Many new converts start out ministering to everyone. But it is not long before we realize that not everyone wants to hear about Jesus. After a few rejections, we are intimidated into silence. Then we begin to lose our joy. Our heart becomes hardened and insensitive to the Lord. Before long we are looking outside of the Kingdom of God for fulfillment.

There is no need for the Christian life to be exciting at first, only to dwindle as time goes by. Our enthusiasm should be greater now than it was when we first believed. But if we deny the fulfillment of our new nature, peace and joy will take wings and fly away.

On the other hand, as one becomes more Christ-like, as the Spirit and the Word of God transform him, ministering becomes more and more a product of who he IS rather than of what he DOES. Because his heart is full of love and excitement for Jesus, it flows out naturally. *"For out of the abundance of the heart the mouth speaketh."* Matthew 12:34.

A witness is someone who has first-hand knowledge of a matter. As you become more familiar with the risen Lord, you cannot help but speak of the things you see and hear. The words you speak and the things you do are an overflow of the abundance of the quality of your life in God. What you do is not compelled by legalism and works, but by love. The more you experience God's love, the more your heart will be changed, and the more you will do what you should do. *"Nevertheless I have somewhat against thee, because thou hast left thy first love. Remember therefore from whence thou art fallen, and repent, and do the first works..."* Revelation 2:4-5.

10

Showing Jesus to the World

Because of unawareness of scriptural purpose, the church has often taken the tools that were given for service and turned inward, thus making the means to the end the end within itself. The gifts of God are not to merely experience but to use.

Isaiah 61:1-3 in the NIV says, *"The Spirit of the Sovereign Lord is on me, because the Lord has anointed me to preach the good news to the poor. He has sent me to bind up the brokenhearted, to proclaim freedom for the captives and release for the prisoners, to proclaim the year of the Lord's favor and the day of vengeance of our God, to comfort all who mourn, and to provide for those who grieve in Zion--to bestow on them a crown of beauty instead of ashes, the oil of gladness instead of mourning, and a garment of praise instead of a spirit of despair. They (speaking of the people who would be ministered to as a result of the Holy Spirit upon Jesus) will be called oaks of righteousness, a planting of the Lord for the display of His splendor."*

As mentioned previously, the Spirit comes in us to give us the new birth and to change our nature.

The Spirit comes upon us to minister to others. This scripture with which Jesus began His public ministry should adequately explain why we have the Spirit of God upon us: to minister life to the lost, the saved, the hurt, the fallen, the forsaken...anyone who needs a higher quality of life. For this purpose, we are empowered by the Holy Spirit.

Since the time of the Reformation, the church has been slowly restored to a scriptural pattern. In recent years there has been a growing awareness of our need for the Holy Spirit and His gifts. However, along with every revelation of truth, there has been a simultaneous abuse. It has been my observation that every move of God has been somewhat thwarted by those who take truth to an extreme. This has been the case with the gifts of the Holy Spirit. The end result has been reproach for anyone who believed in the gifts. Worst of all, they have not been used to touch the world.

For some, the gifts have been presented as a reward for righteousness or holiness, a badge of achievement. For others the gifts are a form of "spiritual entertainment" that takes place in church three times a week. For a few, the gifts of the Holy Spirit have become a means for reaching multitudes of hurting people for the Lord Jesus. They have become a means of alleviating humanity from pain and suffering.

As I have traveled around the world I have seen the most effective missionaries to be those who preach Jesus in the demonstration and power of the Holy Spirit. Paul was committed to proclaiming Jesus in a way that demonstrated God's love for mankind by setting them free from all bondage and oppression. This type of ministry caused men to trust in God and not persuasive arguments. In 1 Corinthians 2:4-5 Paul said, *"And my speech and my preaching was not with enticing words of man's wisdom, but in demonstration of the Spirit and of power: That your faith should not stand in the wisdom of men, but in the power of God."*

We are living in a world that desperately needs to see some reality to our claims. The gifts were not meant to be confined within the walls of the church, but to be tools whereby a lost and dying world would experience the love of God.

Several years ago, the Lord spoke to my heart and said, "The world does not need to hear about me, they need to experience me." Experiencing God is a matter of power. When God's power breaks the yoke of bondage from a person's life, they will believe, and fall in love with Jesus.

Additionally, the Lord said, "The world does not need answers. It needs solutions." All we have offered the world is our answers. The cults have answers; the Satanists have answers; all the religions of the world have answers. The only thing that will separate our answers from their answers will be the power to solve their problems. When those problems are solved, and when those needs are met, they will experience God.

While flying back from the Philippines after a crusade I had an interesting conversation with a "religious" person sitting beside me. I noticed he was reading some type of "religious literature." I was reading my Bible. After a while he asked what I had been doing in the Philippines. When I told him I had been conducting crusades he was surprised. He quickly asked, "Did you have a problem with the Catholic Church while you were there?" "No." I calmly replied. "What about the witch doctors; did they persecute you?" he continued. "Not really," I answered once again. Finally he asked, "Well, who gave you the most opposition?" "No one really opposed us." I fired back. "Well, what makes you different?" came an agitated, half-angry inquiry. I calmly gave my reply, "When you get the sick healed, the blind receive their sight, the cripples walk, and the deaf are healed, people want to hear what you have to say!"

We sat and stared at one another for what seemed like quite a long while. Finally he said, "God does not have to do those things anymore." "Yes." I responded, "But aren't you glad He does, even though He does not have to."

There is not one place in the Bible that says the gifts are over. There is no hint of a special time passing by for the power of God in the earth. If there was ever a time people needed to see the reality of God demonstrated, it is the day in which we live.

Hebrews 1:3 says, *"The Son is the radiance of God's glory and the exact representation of His being..."* (NIV) Besides the fact that Jesus came to be a sacrifice for sin, He also came to show the world what the true God was really like. Jesus said in John 14:9, *"He that hath seen me hath seen the Father; and how sayest thou then, Show us the Father?"* Jesus was God in the flesh. You need not look any farther if you desire to know God. Jesus' entire life was spent doing the will of the Father, so that we might be able to see and know the love of God.

The religious leaders of that day had so distorted and perverted their presentation of God that He was unrecognizable to the world. Jesus said the religious leaders were blind guides. Not only did they lead the blind, but their teachings made them blind. Because of this, He commanded His disciples to leave them alone. *"Let them alone: they are blind leaders of the blind. And if the blind lead the blind, both shall fall into the ditch."* Matthew 15:14. *"Their teachings are but rules taught by men."* Mark 7:7. (NIV)

The religious world was one of tradition. Tradition isolated them from the love and power of God. Jesus said they were making the Word of God of none effect through their tradition, Mark 7:13[1]. But Jesus demonstrated the true God in the way he met the needs of humanity. He not only told them God was love, He demonstrated it through the power of the Holy Spirit. *"For he taught them as one having [authority], and not as the scribes."* Matthew 7:29.

Jesus was not a talker; He was a life giver. Jesus said in John 5:26, *"For as the Father has life Himself, so He has granted the Son to have life in Himself."* Jesus was the exact representation of the life-giving God. Everywhere He went, He carried that life.

In John 17:18 Jesus prayed, *"As you have sent Me into the world, I have sent them into the world."* Yes, just as the Father sent His Son empowered by the Holy Spirit to give life, so the Son sends us empowered by the Holy Spirit. Just as He set the captives free, we are to set the captives free. We have the same commis-

---

[1] *"Making the word of God of no effect through your tradition, which ye have delivered; and many such things do ye."*

sion, purpose and power that Jesus had.

We also live at a time when tradition has perverted the true representation of God. The world does not know God nor have they seen Him. They have only seen the representation the church has shown, and they do not want what they have seen. *"For the name of God is blasphemed among the Gentiles through you, as it is written."* Romans 2:24. For 1800 years, the world has had a very poor representation of God. If we want people to believe in the God of the Bible, we must show them the God of the Bible.

Those who believe in the gifts of the Holy Spirit should be at the forefront of world evangelism. If we believe in the power of God, then we, more than any others, should make ourselves accountable to properly manage what God has given us. We should set the captives free, bind up the brokenhearted, heal the sick, and, yes, do all that Jesus did. We should do it because that same Spirit abides in and upon us. Jesus said it this way, *"I tell you the truth anyone who has faith in Me will do what I have been doing. He will do even greater things than these, because I am going to the Father."* John 14:12. NIV.

As I have studied Jesus' parables, I have found a common denominator among the majority of them: responsibility. When Jesus spoke of stewardship, He was speaking of far more than money management. He was speaking of managing the precious truth and life with which we have been entrusted.

Immediately after Jesus explained that He had come to seek and to save that which was lost in Luke 19:10, Jesus taught the parable of the talents. The parable begins with a commission by the nobleman,

"And he called his ten servants, and delivered them ten pounds, and said unto them, Occupy till I come." Luke 19: 13. The word "occupy" is not passive. It does not mean to hold on to what you have until I get back. It means to be doing business and gaining ground. Most Christians are more interested in "enduring till the end," than in reaching others and gaining ground.

This parable clearly demonstrates the need to use what God has given us to reach others. In comparing Matthew's account with that of Luke's, we see that the servant deceived himself. His excuse was "I was afraid of you. I was afraid I would not do it right. I was afraid to run a risk." But the nobleman pinpointed the real problem in Matthew 25:26. *"His lord answered and said unto him, Thou WICKED and SLOTHFUL servant..."*

Those who embrace the gifts of the Holy Spirit should realize we have been entrusted with much. The gifts of the Holy Spirit are precious and valuable. Let us repent of having buried them in the church for our safekeeping. If this is real, let's take it to the entire world.

When did Jesus' miracles happen? They happened when He was preaching the Word to the lost. He did not insulate Himself from the world to proclaim His truth and demonstrate His power to His disciples alone. No, He carried the Word to those who needed to hear. The Great Commission is to GO PREACHING. The salvation message is not for the church. It is not to be preached Sunday after Sunday. Neither are the miracles to be demonstrated exclusively among the brethren. The gathering of believers is to equip the saints FOR THE WORK OF THE MINISTRY.

As equipped believers go preaching, God confirms His Word with signs and wonders. *"And they went forth, and preached everywhere, the Lord working with them, and confirming the word with signs following. Amen."* Mark 16:20. All the miracles that we, as Spirit-filled believers, long to see will come about when we proclaim the good news of Jesus Christ to a lost world.

"And, behold, I send the promise of my Father upon you: but tarry ye in the city of Jerusalem, until ye be endued with power from on high." Luke 24:49. God never intended for us to go forth without power. Yet, He never intended for us to be empowered and stay home. *"But ye shall receive power, after that the Holy Ghost is come upon you: and ye shall be witnesses unto me both in Jerusalem, and in all Judaea, and in Samaria, and unto the uttermost part of the earth."* Acts 1:8.

While sitting in a large charismatic church one Sunday morning, the Spirit of the Lord began to stir within me. In my heart I could see a soldier dressed in armor. He had on a sword with a shield and all the weapons of war, but instead of being in a battle, he was sitting at a table eating. Then, this word came to me, "No man girds himself up, puts on his armor, taking his sword and shield in his hand and sits down to eat. No, when you gird yourself up in your armor, taking your sword and your shield, you run forth into the battle. Run to the battle, says the Lord. Go forth, for I have equipped you with my weapons of warfare, yet you sit and eat. You desire to be fed more, but I say run forth to the battle."

This particular church, like many, had been

birthed with a vision to reach the city, yet it was not going forth. It was getting fatter and fatter, yet never really reaching forth to fulfil its calling.

If the world is going to see Jesus it will only be as we, the church, show Him. If we do not show and demonstrate God the way Jesus did, then we will never have the results Jesus had. If we do not GO, they will never KNOW. Yet when we go, we must do more than say, we must SHOW.

Every ministry gift of the Spirit is in you because the Spirit Himself is in you. He desires to express the love of God by meeting the needs of the people. as you yield to Him you unleash these gifts (abilities) of the Spirit and the world experiences God.

11

Called to Minister

Catholicism brought about the separation of the clergy and laity. This particular mentality says the average believer cannot be involved in ministry. While we may have doctrinally come out of the Dark Ages; in practice, this mentality still exists. Most believers still look to the pastor or staff members to do the work of the ministry.

Statistics show that neither the pastor nor organized outreach is that effective in reaching the lost. According to one survey: 4-6% of the people in churches today are there because of the pastor. That means a church of 200 people will have between eight and twelve people there as a direct result of the pastor. Despite the pressures that some congregations place on their pastor, it does not require a super-pastor to have a growing church. Additionally, 4-7% of the people in church in America are there because of the Sunday School program. While some consider Sunday School to be the "golden calf" of evangelism, in actuality that same church of 200 people will have between eight and fourteen people as a result of the Sunday School program.

Only 1% of people are there because of church

visitation. Again I am sorry to say, that Monday night visitation will not build you a healthy church. The average church of two hundred now has two people as a result of Monday night visitation.

Mass evangelism brings in less than .001% (one tenth of one percent) of the people. Billy Graham and other evangelistic ministries are quite candid about the low retention of people reached through mass evangelism.

Despite the smallness of these numbers, we should not abandon these types of programs. These programs do meet certain types of needs. They are an essential part of support ministry. Not only do they help to touch people, but also are an excellent training ground for those who desire to develop their ministry skills. But this is not how we really reach people in America.

This same survey revealed that 70-90% of the people in church today are there because of the personal ministry of a friend or relative. We must realize that the masses are saved one at a time, and that we, as individuals, are God's most powerful tool for ministering to the world. There is no substitute for the influence an individual has with his friends and relatives. You are important. God needs you to reach into your family and friends with the gospel. You can reach people no one else will ever reach. Without you, your world may never be won to Jesus.

Ironically, we have come to believe that we cannot reach our family and friends. I have heard it taught that these are the hardest to win. I say, "That is not the truth." Your family and friends can and should be a fruitful field of ministry. If you live a victorious life and maintain a consistent witness, you will have more influence over those closest to you than any other group of people.

In the charismatic movement, with its many strengths, there have been some weaknesses bred into the people. With all the emphasis on submission, anointing, covering and authority, ministry has been taken from the hands of the people and subtly placed in the hands of the clergy. The average believer has, once again, been made to feel that he is somehow too inadequate to accomplish anything significant for God. He has buried his talent in the ground for fear that he may use it the wrong way.

Paul said in Philippians 3:12, "...*I press on to take hold of that for which Christ Jesus took hold of me.*" NIV. Christ took hold of us for a purpose. While there are individual purposes in one's life, each believer must realize that he is called to be a minister. Not only is he called, but an aspect of his new nature longs to be fulfilled by giving life through personal ministry.

There are few happenings to compare with the joy of introducing another person to Jesus and knowing that we can make the eternal difference of heaven or hell in an individual's life. It is a frustration of our nature, a denial of our desire, and a thwarting of our growth to stop that life-giving spring from flowing through us. "*Jesus answered and said unto her, 'Whosoever drinketh of this water shall thirst again; But whosoever drinketh of the water that I shall give him shall never thirst, but the water that I shall give him shall be in him a well of water springing up into everlasting life.' *" John 4:13-14. There is a spring in you that desires to flow out. If it does not come out, it will create a discomfort. It will be a source of discontentment. It will stagnate and bring death.

Apart from fulfilling this need, our power will be limited, our purpose lacking, and personal awareness of the good things of God will be deficient. However, when one yields to the life-giving aspect of his nature, he opens himself to new dimensions of the Spirit's activity. Reaching out prevents reaching in. As we give of what we have received, new life from God flows in. As we share our faith we begin to move in new areas of faith.

Never let anyone rob you of your individual call to minister. You may not be mature, you may not even be stable, but if you know you are saved, you have a testimony. Because you have first hand evidence that Jesus is raised from the dead, you are qualified to be a witness. (Please, live a life that is a testimony, so you will not bring reproach to the gospel.)

When I was first saved, I had no church background. I was not raised in church. I knew very little about God. I went directly home and began to read the New Testament. I told God I would not play church, and I would only believe what I saw in the Bible with my own eyes.

I sat in a rocking chair in my living room for days. All I did was read the Bible and pray. Within a few days I had read the entire New Testament from cover to cover. In that period of time I was baptized in the Holy Spirit. I knew that I needed to be baptized in water, so I went to church.

I met a man who took me under his "wing." He

was a deacon in the church and fortunately was not extremely traditional. I told him of my desire to win others to Jesus. We devised a plan to bring a group of hippies and musicians into my home. When I got them together, he told them about Jesus.

It all looked easy enough to me, so I began contacting all my old friends and telling them about my experience. Some thought I was crazy, some thought drugs had finally damaged my mind, but some wanted what I had found in Jesus.

I went to a local Youth for Christ center and shared my testimony with the director. He took me into the schools to share my testimony. I was not a good speaker, and I, by no means, had all of my problems solved; but I seized every opportunity to share the gospel.

As my boldness grew, I began witnessing one-on-one on the streets. I saw great revival on the streets in those days. I might add, every time I saw someone get saved, my confidence in the power of the gospel multiplied. My boldness was not in me, but it was in the power of the gospel.

I would look in the paper to see what was showing at the local theater. When I would find something that made people think of spiritual things such as movies about demons, life after death, etc., I would go to that theater and witness to people as they were coming out. Because of what they had just seen, they were very receptive.

On one occasion I witnessed to a group of men. They formed a circle around me as I talked. I was not sure what was about to happen; I thought they were going to attack me. When I reached a place to pray with them, they all dropped to their knees, right on the sidewalk, with people walking all around. They all prayed to receive Jesus as their Lord.

In those early days I made so many mistakes. I misquoted verses. I was out in left field on some of my theology. But, I was saved and did not mind telling people about it. I can remember being criticized for my zeal. I was told it would not last. I had every opportunity to be discouraged, but I turned a deaf ear to the voice of criticism and kept sharing Jesus.

On Friday and Saturday nights, I would prowl the streets and witness until two or three o'clock in the morning. Because I was out so late I did not go to Sunday School, but I was always there in time for the worship service. I remember one Sunday School teacher who commented, "I could never be supportive of a ministry like that. He does not even attend Sunday School regularly." Now this man would have had me in a Sunday School class learning instead of out on the streets ministering.

By all means, get training. I am president of a Bible college. I, more than most, believe in the need to prepare. However, all Bible training should be done hand-in-hand with practical application. While you are learning about eschatology, you should be getting people ready to meet Jesus. While you are learning about hell, you should be preventing souls from going. While you are learning about the gifts of the Spirit, you should be letting them flow through your life. While you are learning about homiletics, you should be preaching to the lost. Do not ever stop ministering.

As I have studied the book of Acts, I have seen that the world was actually reached by the believers, not the apostles. The apostles were obviously used to do some mighty things. They saw some powerful mass evangelism. But the world was turned upside down by the disciples.

The five-fold ministry should equip you, but that equipping should encourage you to minister. Our preaching and teaching should never limit and restrict the disciples from ministry.

You may never preach on the streets, knock on doors or stand in a pulpit, but you will have more exposure to humanity than any preacher. The people you work with may never hear your pastor, but they can hear you. They may not trust the tele-evangelist, but they trust you. It is your family, friends and business associates over which you have the most influence. Handle these opportunities as precious treasures, for they are YOUR "talents."

The following will help you develop a natural approach to ministry. Do not think you will minister to people the way a preacher ministers behind a pulpit. Always minister from the overflow. Read the Bible, pray, worship, go to church and have a good relationship with the Lord. The more God is real to you, the more naturally you will speak of Him. IT IS WHO YOU ARE, NOT WHAT YOU DO. If you stay full of the Spirit, what you have will spill over onto others. Remember the Scripture says you are salt and you are light. Every believer is some kind of light. You are either a bright light, clearly showing the way or a dim light making the way hard to distinguish. Concentrate on being what you should be, then the doing takes very little effort.

Learn to be **conversational**. The old method of

"nailing someone" does not produce a very productive response. Practice being friendly. Introduce yourself to people. Take the initiative. If you do not know what to say, let them do the talking. As a matter of fact, most people will think that you are more interesting if you let them do the talking. I get people talking by asking questions about their family, occupation and recreation.

As they open up, they begin to feel a trust. Conversation brings the walls down. Out on the street, this is impossible. But in our daily environment, it is essential. Always remember, the people you will win and keep will be those who know you. Street ministry actually puts very few people in churches, but it does teach believers how to effectively witness. It is a place of facing and overcoming fears.

I had to learn to be conversational. I am good at talking if I have something in particular to say. But I am not good at small talk. So I developed the ability to ask questions and allow others to speak, then I began to see more success.

Humor is an excellent way to help people become open and relaxed. If you have the ability to be funny and make people laugh, you have a powerful tool. On one occasion, I went in a fast food restaurant. When they rang up my order I asked, "Did you figure in my discount?" I was dressed in a nice suit and tie. The girl looked me over and replied, "I did not know how to do that." She called another girl over and said, "I forgot to figure in his discount." They both looked at the cash register and the receipt in total despair. They called the manager out and said, "We have already rung up the order and we forgot to figure in his discount." As she looked at me with a puzzled look, I began to laugh. After we all had a good laugh, I gave them all a tract and shared Jesus with them. I have had many situations where humor and friendliness opened the door for the ministry.

Learn to recognize and seize **every opportunity**. We need not pray for opportunities, we are surrounded by opportunity. We must, however, develop sensitivity to recognize the needs of others around us. Our real areas of effectiveness are those places where we conduct daily affairs: the grocery store, the service station or any place where you come in contact with people.

While flying back from a business meeting I became stranded in an airport. The previous flight had been canceled. Now there were two planeloads of people trying to get on the next flight out. Because of technical problems, that flight was delayed. People were mad, swearing and arguing. i prayed, "Lord, if I want to be effective, help me to be sensitive."

I found a seat and began reading. I happened to glance over at a lady in another seat. She was reading a book that had an interesting title. I asked her about her book, and then I asked her where she was from. I asked about family and occupation. (I did this in a way that seemed friendly, not nosey.)

Soon she began to ask me questions. When she asked me about my occupation I replied, "I am a preacher." She looked me over and said, "You do not look much like a preacher." I replied, "A lot of people say that. What do you think a preacher should look like?" We both began to laugh. Then she stated, "I am Catholic."

I never let her draw me into a religious debate. I simply followed the lead she had given me. I began to talk about the mold that had been created for preachers and Christians. This gave me the opportunity to begin to talk about the heart as opposed to the appearance. Before long I was able to introduce her to the fact that God wanted to change our heart. He did not want us living in law and bondage.

By this time, everyone within hearing distance was listening to our conversation. I went through "Creation to Calvary" and asked if there was any reason that she could not make Jesus Lord. She gave an uncomfortable glance at the people who were obviously listening. We stepped into another area that was a little more private. Together we bowed our heads, and she invited Jesus into her life as Lord.

We are all surrounded by these opportunities. All of us must remind ourselves of our purpose and pursue it, or these opportunities will come and go without our ever knowing it. We are all ministers, the world is our pulpit and the problems are our invitations to minister.

Because of familiarity and routine, we do not expect anything to happen in these places. Or, because we are so absorbed in the cares of this life, we have become insensitive. Regardless of the reason, we are surrounded by opportunities that come and go without ever doing anything.

When people complain, have problems or ask questions, we should turn these into opportunities. We should pray daily for sensitivity to the needs of those around us. Remember, behind every problem or weakness is always a need.

We are called to proclaim the gospel, not explain it. Just the simple plan of salvation or a word of personal testimony is sufficient. God does not need theologians, just witnesses. God's promises received with faith will suffice for any situation.

When people ask questions that you cannot answer, do not get nervous. Keep them on the track you do know. Often someone will ask me a theological question. If I perceive it to be a defense mechanism, I usually respond with something like this, "You can learn about that anytime. I want to talk to you about Jesus." Or, "Knowing the answer to that question will not help you find the solution to your problem, let's stick to the most important things."

You should always have a plan. Be familiar with a few scripture passages that will clearly explain the new birth, healing and other special needs. Memorize and be able to discuss them. Romans 10:9-10 is the most essential of all scriptures for soul winning. Actually, believing that God raised Jesus from the dead is the key to every promise of God.

We teach people to use a simple method for soul winning we call "Creation to Calvary," which is spelled out in another chapter. We have found it to be simple, concise and quite effective. Whatever your plan, let it be full of love and compassion, free from judgement and condemnation. Make sure it brings people to a point of decision.

Last of all; always ask for a commitment. This is where most people fall apart. Some will do a great presentation of Jesus. But when it is time to actually ask for a commitment, we get weak at the knees. For the most part it is time to harvest not plant the seed.

Do not be afraid to share the plan of salvation and then lead them in a prayer of commitment to the Lord. Lay hands on the sick and pray for them. Whatever you do, always bring people to a clear decision. The Word is of no value until those who hear it mix it with faith. Calling for an action will stimulate the person to make a clear-cut decision.

Never be "pushy" in asking for a commitment. As I have said before, I simply ask, "Is there any reason you could not confess Jesus as Lord?" Regardless of their reasons, I usually reply with something like, "All of those things are important, but none of them are important enough to keep you out of heaven." Then I simply ask, "Would you rather pray yourself or would you rather I lead you in a prayer?"

You will find that people will love and appreciate you for sharing Jesus with them. If you do it in love, you will seldom have people offended and angry. Do not let any fear hinder you from opening your mouth and sharing the goodness of the Lord.

Only as the individual church members rise up and fulfill their call will we experience real revival. It is up to the people to minister to the needs of their community. You are the key to revival in your church. Do not allow anything to keep you from the most important thing you will ever do for God...BEING A MINISTER.

12

Why Christians Do Not Minister

Different statistics reveal the attitude of the church in evangelism. One report says the average Christian only leads one person to Christ every 33 years. Other statistics reflect the same apathy. Why would people who have been forgiven of so much, fail to share with others? The answers are as various as there are different kinds of people. But there are a few simple reasons that appeal to the majority.

People follow the pattern they are shown. In many cases people were saved because they got so desperate they started going to church. They were saved at a church; therefore, they think everyone will get saved at church. When the focus of ministry is Sunday services, we establish a limiting paradigm.

This pattern of thought is reaffirmed when pastors fail to encourage and train believers to reach out to others. Because many pastors are easily threatened at the thought of one-on-one ministry, they are unable to impart this vision to the people.

Pastors who have a lack of experience with one-on-one often encourage our fears of ministry.

Some pastors unknowingly pass their fears of personal ministry on to the people in the form of teachings that complicate or misrepresent personal ministry.

It is essential that a pastor who is not strong in personal ministry have a staff evangelist that trains and leads the people in outreach ministry. Since it is the work of the five-fold ministry to equip the saints for the work of the ministry, the evangelist must train them in personal ministry. To have a staff evangelist is not a sign of weakness, but of wisdom. The pastor's hands will be quite full if he pastors the people. It would be too idealistic to expect the pastor to do every job.

Traditionally, we have considered the evangelist to be one who travels and holds meetings in churches. Thereby, we have robbed the church of this precious gift. The evangelist working through a local church can be the source of continual new life in the church. Souls will be won, excitement will be high, and there will be continuous opportunities to train new leaders as church members work in areas of personal ministry. The evangelist should develop the church in personal ministry.

Through the various outreaches of the church such as prisons, street ministry, hospitals, nursing homes, follow-up, cell ministry, etc., a church will give those with a call the opportunity to be trained and use their gift. The benefits of this are multiple. It wins souls; it trains leaders, it meets needs and reduces division by giving ministry opportunity to those who are called. Additionally, it gives the church a tremendous sense of purpose.

Overcomplicating is another common cause of believers not ministering. When a leader is not confident in personal ministry, he will complicate its presentation to the people. Most of us have been led to believe that we must know how to answer every possible question, we must memorize dozens of scriptures, understand all the complexities of Christian life and have a special anointing before we can minister.

In actuality, it is **new** converts that win the most people to the Lord. A witness is not a theologian; a witness is one who has first hand knowledge of the facts. The new convert just knows he is saved, and he's glad of it and excited. Excitement draws far more people to Christ than theology. Theology is the basis of debate. Love, mercy and the message of Jesus are the basis for exciting ministry.

Disqualification is the most common reason for the lack of personal ministry. I am continually amazed at the number of people who really want to do something for God, but they have been convinced that they are not yet mature enough. Leaders tend to think one must be faultless for God to use them. If that is the case, all the preachers I know, including myself, had better step out of the pulpit.

This disqualification is very destructive. It destroys the new believer's self-confidence. It makes him introspective and critical of himself. It will eventually make him critical of everyone. He will be forced to begin to compare himself with others. He will look for faults in others and will find them. This will ultimately undermine his confidence in leadership, in the church and even his salvation experience. Active ministry, on the other hand, will produce love, compassion, maturity and mercy as it flows through us to the people.

Unbelief in the power of the gospel is another

common contributor. Paul said in Romans 1:16, *"...The gospel of Christ...is the power of God unto salvation to everyone that believeth..."* Since the gospel has been overcomplicated to us, we have been robbed of confidence in its power.

A lack of confidence in the gospel will move one into explaining rather than proclaiming. In 1 Corinthians 1:17 Paul says it this way, *"For Christ sent me not to baptize, but to preach the gospel: not with wisdom of words, lest the [cross] of Christ should be made of none effect."* When we begin to explain the cross, we move into this area of the "wisdom of words." When we do this, we make the cross of none effect.

People are not called to understand the gospel; they are called to believe it. Understanding will not produce life, salvation, healing and victory. However, believing will. Because we feel the need to explain, the burden to produce results falls on our shoulders. We start trying to develop eloquence instead of faith.

The Holy Spirit works with the Word. By speaking the Word of God, we give someone the opportunity to believe. Sharing the message of the cross is what the Spirit works with to bring a person to experience every aspect of salvation. When we share what Jesus did at the cross, the Holy Spirit can touch their hearts and bring them to healing, salvation or repentance. In doing so, the burden to produce is on the Holy Spirit leaving me with only the burden to proclaim.

One important factor in having confidence and power to witness is the baptism in the Holy Spirit. Jesus told his disciples to tarry in Jerusalem until they were endued with power from on high. Contrary to Pentecostal opinion, the baptism in the Holy Spirit is not something one achieves by reaching a level of holiness. The baptism in the Holy Spirit is not only a promise to everyone who believes, but it is a commandment for everyone who believes.

The primary purpose of the baptism in the Holy Spirit is to make every believer a witness that can operate in the power of God. Acts 1:8 says, *"But ye shall receive power, after that the Holy Ghost is come upon you: and ye shall be [witnesses] unto me..."* If we are giving testimony to the gospel, we must do it with power, otherwise all we have is an argument. We have already seen that the arguments and wisdom of words rob the cross of power. In another chapter we will discuss the full scope of ministry which operates in the power of God.

The last reason for a lack of personal witnessing is hardness of heart. Hardness of heart plagued the disciples. In Mark 6:52, we see the disciple's heart problem was the result of what they considered or thought. They did not think on things above, and they did not think about the miracles. Their hearts were hardened by what they thought about. They looked at the problem, not the promise. Only a close, intimate relationship will keep our hearts soft and pliable before the Lord.

A life of fruitful prayer and devotion in the Word makes one's heart sensitive to the things of God. Since we become like those we fellowship with, it is impossible to fellowship with God and not develop a heart for ministry. When Jesus isolated Himself with God, He always emerged in powerful ministry.

The scripture in Acts 1:8 said, "*...you would BE witnesses.*" This is more than something you do; it is what you are. The heart for the world is only developed in personal communion with the Lord. In our School of Ministry we teach the "overflow principle." If you fill your heart with God to capacity, it will start to overflow. Ministry will not be something you make yourself do, but it will flow forth from what you are.

The Bible says in Luke 6:45, "*A good man out of the good treasure of his heart bringeth forth that which is good; and an evil man out of the evil treasure of his heart bringeth forth that which is evil: for of the abundance of the heart his mouth speaketh.*" What we can comfortably bring forth from our mouth is the product of our heart. Therefore, intimacy with God, falling in love with the Father, and being full of the Spirit and Word is the best way to BE a witness.

Fear of rejection is probably the most common constraint in personal ministry. Proverbs 29:25 says, "*The fear of man bringeth a snare: but whoso putteth his trust in the Lord shall be safe.*" When I was first saved, I told everyone about Jesus. For a while most of the people tolerated me, but it was not long until some of them began to attack me. When I was rejected for my beliefs, it affected my eagerness to witness.

I went to talk to a preacher about my dilemma. I did not realize this man had never witnessed to anyone. He gave me what sounded like some very wise advice. "Now, not everyone wants to hear what has happened to you. Do not let your excitement turn them off to the Lord." He had developed a theology that gave him comfort for not winning souls. I am so glad I did not listen to him.

The world is already turned off. If we give the gospel in love, we might turn them on. The gospel does not turn anybody off. If you present it in a negative way, you might turn them off. But people are ready to hear. The truth is that we, the Christians, are the ones who are turned off. We are afraid of damaging our fragile self-worth. We are turned off to the needs of the world.

One of the deepest needs in a man is the need for self-worth. A man will go to any length to preserve self-worth or self-esteem. Few people ever conquer this snare. However, as one builds an intimate relationship with the Lord, the love and compassion of God will motivate his actions. Through intimacy, a Biblical self-worth is established in the Lord Jesus. A strong sense of Biblical self-worth has no fear of man.

In every job situation I have had, people were led to the Lord. I did not attack or preach, but the way I did business created conversation. In business meetings, I would reference my remarks with "the Bible says." I would talk about the Lord as if they were believers. Because I was comfortable talking about these things, they were comfortable. As often as not, they would stimulate the conversations that would result in their salvation.

If this is what I AM, I never feel awkward trying to DO. This will keep you from the "soul winning syndrome." This syndrome makes you feel responsible to win the whole world. You feel so much condemnation and pressure to minister that you become awkward and confused, which makes everyone else feel awkward. You will spend your days looking for just the right moment and always wondering if you missed it. When Jesus is the center of your life, you cannot help but talk about Him. It will be natural, joyful and fruitful. Those who hear you and desire what you have will express their interest. The Bible says to be ready to give an answer to everyone that asks...We need to live a life that causes people to ask.

13

Sanctifying Jesus in Your Heart

The number one priority when preparing for ministry is sanctifying (setting apart) Jesus in your own heart. The relationship you have with Jesus is more important than any other single factor. 1 Peter 3:15 says, *"But sanctify the Lord God in your hearts, and be ready always to give an answer to every man that asketh you a reason of the hope that is in you, with meekness and fear..."* There is nothing more important than your personal relationship with Jesus.

Every worthwhile thing in your life will be birthed from your personal relationship with the Lord Jesus. Apart from a living, loving relationship with God, works, witnessing and ministering will be something you do as an attempt to please the Lord.

With the works mentality, we tend to determine our worth by what we do, rather than by who we are. This is a horrible travesty of truth. It is this very mentality that turns serving the Lord with gladness into serving the Lord with frustration.

Our worth should be based totally on the finished work of Jesus. It is not based on our works or accomplishments. As one enters into an intimate personal relationship with the Lord, He shares that love and acceptance with us. He speaks intimately and confirms our heart. Psalms 112:7 speaks of the man who (reverently, worshipfully) fears the Lord. It says, *"He shall not be afraid of evil tidings; his heart is fixed, trusting in the LORD."*

Worship and intimacy turn truth into life, and fellowship and trust turn doctrine into personal words. It is in personal communion that the Lord turns the commission into compassion. Personal communion with the Lord is what removes one from the realm of doing into the realm of being. Thus, the best preparation for being an effective witness, minister, singer or anything in the Kingdom, is the relationship you have with the Lord.

NEVER, EVER GAIN PERSONAL WORTH FROM WORKS. Proverbs 4:23 warns, *"Keep* (guard) *thy heart with all diligence; for out of it are the issues of life."* Let all that you do be a product of who you are and what you experience in Jesus. Jesus wants you to BE a witness, not merely DO witnessing. In Matthew 5:13, 14, Jesus said, *"...ye are salt...ye are light..."* What we are determines the effect we have on people.

In fact, we are all some kind of light. We may be a bright light that shines before men clearly showing the love and goodness of the Lord, or we may be a dim light that causes men to stumble and fall. Be assured, what we are speaks far louder than what we do.

I remember hearing a story about a man out witnessing on the streets. He walked up to one man and said, "Would you like to read this tract about Jesus?" The man replied, "I can't read so I will just follow in your tracks." People should be able to follow us and live in victory. Our life should be the strongest witness we have.

1 Peter 3:16 says, *"Having a good conscience, that, whereas they speak evil of you, as of evildoers, they may be ashamed that falsely accuse your good conversation in Christ."* Even when men are against us and accuse us, our life should make them ashamed.

Being a witness is a life-changing commitment. What you do can be done occasionally, but what you are is continuous. Being a minister is the end of living for self. It is entering into a realm where you live to give. Your entire life revolves around a purpose. This does not mean you will flag down every person you see. You will not be waiving tracts in everybody's face. You will not attack every service station attendant and grocery clerk, but you will be ever alert to needs in the lives of others. You will learn to live for a cause beyond yourself.

The ability to do this without entering the realm of the bizarre is a product of a good relationship with Jesus. People fear that a commitment to personal ministry will condemn them to a life where they have to shave their head, wear a sheet and pass out tracts in the airport. In actuality, it will bring forth love and compassion that will not only make you sensitive to the needs of others, it will attract others to you.

We cannot please everyone, and we cannot live in fear of what anyone thinks. But one who has a heart for ministry will determine his dress, hair, manners, conversation and entire life in light of the needs of others. Do not mistake this strength for codependent weakness that seeks to win the approval of others. This is simply a committed, responsible lifestyle that is able to make choices free from selfish motives.

The church has tried to legalize this type of commitment by developing standards of holiness and rules of conduct. All of these laws simply become a yoke that crushes the Christian and turns the world away from God. You are not earning God's approval to be a minister. If you are in Jesus, you have God's approval. Realizing God's love and approval becomes a basis for ministering love and acceptance to others.

There is only one way to live a sanctified life without entering into law and that is to sanctify Jesus in your own heart. Being in love with Jesus is the answer. We will only grow into this kind of love when we know and believe His great love for us. The apostle John said it this way, *"We know and believe the love God has for us."* (TLB) Let us live our life in a way that helps others believe and experience that love.

14

Ready to Give an Answer

1 Peter 3:15 says, *"But sanctify the Lord God in your hearts, and be ready always to give an answer to every man that asketh you a reason of the hope that is in you, with meekness and fear..."* The result of sanctifying Jesus in our heart is always pleasant. A relationship with Jesus is the ground from which the fruit of the Spirit can grow in our hearts. This is what draws people to us.

One of the greatest misconceptions of personal ministry is that we have to aggressively pursue people for ministry. This is the doomed plight of the angry legalist. Nothing could be farther from the truth, however, for the person who feels and expresses the love of God.

Although I have done much street evangelism, the most effective ministry for me has always been people that were drawn to me. A recent survey gave some startling statistics about why people are in church. We have minimized our ability to reach and keep the masses. We have thought we had to be street preachers, pastors or missionaries to have the greatest effect, but that is far from the truth. The best results come from believers who live a victorious life and minister to their friends and family. It is not super preachers, super evangelists or super television programs that are reaching and keeping the masses of people. Those are myths that have been perpetuated by the religious community.

While I have great value for those who labored during the "healing revival," some sources indicate that the healing revival made very little impact on our nation. It is not really the high profile preacher who makes the greatest impact.

So, where do the people come from? What gets them saved, into church and walking with God? It is the people they know and work with, people they have fun with, and people to whom they are related. We have been convinced that our family and friends will be the hardest to minister to because they know us and live with us. That is the fact, they get to see Jesus change us. They know how "crummy" we were before Jesus helped us. If they see a change in our life, they will want to know what it is. For this reason 70-90% of all the people in churches today are there because of the personal influence of a friend or relative.

All of the programs are good; we should not discard any of our efforts. But all of our programs should be designed to train people to go home and minister effectively. They should never replace the role of the average believer in day-to-day life.

In his book "*More Than Numbers*," Dr. Cho states that the homogeneous factor is the most powerful obstacle in reaching people. People are influenced by their social peers. This influence is not realized because you preach to them, but because you live in front of them. When others see you living in victory, enduring hardships and walking in love, they will want to know how you do it.

Peter said be ready to give an answer to everyone that ASKS the reason of the hope that is in you. If no one is ASKING, they must not be SEEING anything. The majority of the world is unsatisfied; most people do not enjoy their work. It has been reported that a large percentage of people would not remarry the same person if they had the choice. Likewise, the majority of people are not satisfied with their present employment. Our society has led a godless, self-centered life that has reaped nothing but pain and emptiness. When they see someone who has peace and joy, they will respond.

The initial response of the world may not be positive. They do not believe it is real. So they will put you to the test. 1 Peter 3:14 says this, *"But and if ye suffer for righteousness' sake, happy are ye; and be not afraid of their terror, neither be troubled."* 1 Peter 4:14 continues, *"If ye be reproached for the name of Christ, happy are ye; for the Spirit of glory and of God resteth upon you; on their part he is evil spoken of, but on your part he is glorified."* Before the world trusts this, they want to be sure it is real. Everything else they have tried has fallen apart. Do not be surprised when they put you to the test.

I have often been cursed, verbally abused and ostracized for being a believer. Very often, however, those who persecuted me became the ones who asked the questions. Once they see it is real, they want it. Additionally, the more they persecute you, the more guilt they feel because of their actions. When they show you the devil, you show them Jesus. Your love and patience is the proof of faith.

The world will either reject or receive Jesus in you. If you have filled your heart with Jesus, they will see Him in you. They will see Him in the way you react to pressure, problems and difficulty. They do not care how you react when things are going right; they want to know if it works in the midst of turmoil.

Some of the people I have had the greatest effect on were the ones who persecuted me FOR RIGHTEOUSNESS SAKE. Most Christians do not suffer for being righteous; they suffer for being critical, judgmental and poor employees. 1 Peter 2:20 says it this way, *"For what glory is it, if, when ye be buffeted for your faults, ye shall take it patiently? But if, when ye do well and suffer for it, ye take it patiently, this is acceptable with God."*

We should be model employees. We should always be the peacemakers and we should be the standard of excellence in all we do. When we live this life, the world will see the real Jesus in us. When they are sure this is real, they will ask. All the street witnessing, one-on-one and visitation is valuable training for ministry, but more than anything, having our hearts full of Jesus will prepare us to give them the reason for our hope.

The word "hope" means "confident expectation of good." Every Christian who is filled with the love of God should be bubbling over with hope. Because the world has lost hope, it is turning to every perversion, drug and entertainment to placate the despair. Real satisfaction only comes, however, when the Jesus in you gets into them.

When there is a conflict between verbal and

non-verbal communication, people always believe the non-verbal. Our lifestyle, the way we treat others, must be consistent with our words. Long after people forget what you say, they will remember how you made them feel.

Because we are the Bible people read and the Jesus people see, we must understand the power of our lifestyle. Titus 2:10 says, "*...showing all good fidelity, that they may adorn the doctrine of God, our Savior in all things.*" The NIV says it this way, "*in every way...make the teaching about God our Savior attractive.*" Our lifestyle should make the gospel attractive. Regardless of what we say, people will usually only believe what they see. The world needs to see enough of Jesus flowing out of us to want Him.

Personal ministry is by far the most powerful, effective and enduring. Never minimize the effect of your life. Let people who will not hear your words about Jesus experience the love of God through your words and actions. People may argue with your doctrine of God's love, but they will let you show them God's love.

When I was first saved, the majority of my friends totally deserted me. They wanted nothing to do with me. My best friend never came to my house or spoke to me after he heard about my becoming a Christian. Rumors were spread that I had overdosed on drugs and had lost my mind. None of that mattered in light of the joy that was mine. I was so glad to be saved that I did not care.

Now, nearly twenty years later, I have won many of those people to Jesus. Every member of my immediate family is saved, and my family was not an easy group to win. Most of those people did not listen to my words; they watched my life. When they believed it was real, they asked.

During the years, I often came under condemnation because I was not more aggressive with my family. But the Lord always gave me the grace to stay on track. They had to see it working in me and they had to experience the love of the Lord through me.

If I had become "preachy" or pushy, they would have been turned off. They all knew how sorry I was before I got saved. They just watched and asked questions. I was never shy about sharing Jesus with them, but I always tried to do it in love and kindness. I wanted to show them a Jesus they could love.

One of the greatest tools you will ever have to win the lost will be your family. People in America are so lonely. Heartbreak is a way of life. Most people do not believe there are actually happy families any more. When people come into my home, they do not see perfect children, perfect parents or perfect anything. What they do see, however, is a lot of love and joy.

This environment draws people to our home. We rarely sit down to eat without guests. While this has been very trying for my wife, and somewhat taxing on my budget, it has been a tremendous place of ministry.

People always ask what we do to have such a happy family. When they ask, the door is open to share Jesus. Even people who are saved receive a great deal of personal ministry as a result of our family life.

If we are salt, we should make the world thirsty. If we are light, we should draw people out of the darkness. Always live a life that makes people ask.

15

Sacrifice: The Heart of Ministry

"And when he had called the people unto him with his disciples also, he said unto them, Whosoever will come after me, let him deny himself, and take up his cross, and follow me. For whosoever would save his life shall lose it; but whosoever shall lose his life for my sake and the gospel's, the same shall save it." Mark 8:34-35. The only pathway to a full and abundant life is sacrifice of self for the purposes of God.

The Expositors Commentary says this should be translated as, "Whoever wills to be first must will (be willing) to be last." There is nothing wrong with having a will or desire to be first if one is willing to be a servant to get there.

The life of sacrifice is foreign to all we have been taught and all we have learned from our old nature. We think we must fulfill our personal desires to be happy, but that only leads to deeper self-centeredness, which leads to less peace and joy. It is a syndrome that dominates the lives of every unhappy person who has ever lived.

Proverbs 18:2 says, *"A fool hath no delight in*

understanding, but that his heart may discover itself."
The fool is always longing to find (discover) himself.
His search for self is always sought down the pathway
of self-centeredness. This is a never-ending search
since it never produces joy.

The refusal to live for something other than self
is at the heart of all our problems. Not only does it
prevent ministry, but also steals personal joy and
peace. The only way to live is to die and the only way
to be exalted is to humble oneself. Jesus said it this
way, "*...whoever shall lose his life for my sake and the
gospel's the same shall save it.*" Mark 8:35.

The Biblical concept of sacrifice does not mean
we cannot fulfill our desires. It does, however, mean
that we cannot violate the law of love to do so. God
wants to fulfill your desires. He wants you happy and
fulfilled. But, that can never happen when we selfishly
pursue our desires. If I trust Him to fulfill my desires,
then I do not have to be consumed by them. I have the
emotional freedom to look beyond myself and minister
to the needs of others.

Jesus was our perfect example of victory, peace
and joy. If anyone had a right to be depressed, frustrated and angry, it would have been Him. He had
never sinned, yet He would die for every man's sin. To
add insult to injury, those for whom He would die
would reject him, but He was never angry or depressed.
His joy was in doing the will of the Father. Remember
that we partake of what we allow to flow through us.
Jesus continually partook of that divine love that
flowed out through Him.

Philippians 2:5-9 says, "*Let this mind be in you,
which was also in Christ Jesus, Who, being in the form*

of God, thought it not robbery to be equal with God, But made himself of no reputation, and took upon him the form of a servant, and was made in the likeness of men, And, being found in fashion as a man, he humbled himself and became obedient unto death, even the death of the cross. Wherefore, God also hath highly exalted him..." We are to have the same mind or attitude as Jesus. He chose to humble Himself and become a servant. In so doing, He always had joy, victory and peace.

We cannot have the victory Jesus had if we do not have the same attitudes and opinions. When we see that humility and servanthood are the road to exaltation, it becomes a joy instead of a job. God has the ability to exalt us far above our means. Psalms 75:6-7 identifies God as the source of promotion: "*For promotion cometh neither from the east, nor from the west, nor from the south. But God is the judge; he putteth down one, and setteth up another.*" The road to exaltation is found in the life of Jesus. "*The disciple is not above his master, nor the servant above his lord.*" Matthew 10:24. "*But he that is greatest among you shall be your servant.*" Matthew 23:11. "*Blessed is that servant, whom his lord, when he cometh, shall find so doing.*" Matthew 24:46. "*So after he had washed their feet, and had taken his garments, and was set down again, he said unto them, Know ye what I have done to you? Ye call me Master and Lord; and ye say well; for so I am. If I, then, your Lord and Master, have washed your feet, ye also ought to wash one another's feet.*" John 13:12-14.

Jesus never fought to exalt Himself, yet He was exalted above every name. Jesus never took from others, however, His needs were always met. Jesus lived a life of total sacrifice and fulfillment. His fulfillment came from the Father because He chose to empty Himself. He made a sacrifice by choice, not by force.

James 4:6 tells us, *"God gives grace to the humble."* Grace is God's ability that works in us. Once we choose to humble ourselves, God gives us the ability and strength to put truth into practice. Simply make a choice that you will LIVE TO GIVE! Ask the Lord for the grace and then do it. Grace (God's ability) will come as you walk it out.

How do you get this on a practical level? Where do you start applying this? Start with this motto, "I will make you glad that you met me." That should be the attitude with which we meet a new person or situation. A servant is ever looking for an opportunity to serve. I am not talking about being a "mushy," "fake" Christian, but meeting real needs and having genuine concern. You make someone glad they met you by helping them meet a need in their life by encouragement, leading them in salvation, casting out their devils, getting them healed or, in short, helping them experience God's love. I am not speaking of a humanitarian mentality. I am talking about ministering the life and love of God to people. I am talking about moving in faith and power to set them free from every hurtful, destructive force. It is this very attitude that unleashes the gifts and power of God.

The best way to find a person's need is not by asking. You usually find someone's need when they expose their faults. Behind every fault, there is a need. Self-centered people are usually offended by the faults of others; therefore, they are incapable of helping them.

Keep in mind, everyone who needs help has a problem. I have actually heard people say, "I would like to help him, but he's got so many problems." That is the point of ministry. He does have problems, and those problems are a reflection of the need in his life.

Love and acceptance expressed in the face of an unlovable attitude has an unbelievable power. That is exactly what God has done for us. 1 John 4:10 says, *"Herein is love, not that we loved God, but that he loved us, and sent his Son to be the propitiation for our sins."* God loved us and expressed that love in the face of rejection. It is the power of that love that draws sinners to repentance. God's love shown to those who have needs is what draws them to repentance.

When you meet someone, ask yourself, "How can I help? What can I do now? What is the real need?" The Lord will open to you some very practical ways to be a servant. The love you pour out will permeate your life, and God will exalt you. Mark 10:43-45 says, *"But so shall it not be among you: but whosoever will be great among you, shall be your minister: And whosoever of you will be the chiefest, shall be servant of all. For even the Son of man came not to be ministered unto, but to minister, and to give his life a ransom for many."* When you live to give, you have found the heart of God and the heart of ministry.

I remember once receiving a call from a bitter lady. She was wounded in a divorce. Her finances were tight and, in general, she was mad at the world. She began to complain about not having friends. "Nobody ever invites me to their house. People do not seem to want to be around me, but you and Brenda always have friends," she complained.

I began to explain the concept of being a servant. Opening your home to people, not so they could meet your need, but that you might meet theirs. She snapped back, "That is easy for you to do, but I do not have the money to feed people like you do."

What she did not know was that I did not have the money. When we fed people, we were often giving our last food. In fact, there were times she had helped eat all we had. God always provided. There were times we had to "tighten our belts," but we never starved.

She never would receive what I had to say. She thought it was a little harder for her to sacrifice than it was for anyone else. Like most, she lived by the concept, "When God gives me everything I want, then I will do something for others." While this seems logical, it is a mask for self-centered justification.

Take what you have now and use it for God. Like Jesus, take the few fish and bread you have and God will multiply it. The exciting part is that you get to eat the fish and loaves that you serve.

In the early days, our family had almost no money and had extreme hardship, but we had all the joy and love anyone could ever want. People crowded into our little apartment by the dozens to receive the Word and ministry. We were tired a lot; our phone rang a little too much; and we did not have a great amount of privacy. There were those who came to take advantage, but we had what everyone wanted.

My family has sacrificed for the gospel. My children have grown up with people in our home. The price has been tremendous, but the dividends have been indescribable.

16

Take Them to Church

Nothing is ever done without some kind of a plan. I am not saying that ministry only happens when there is a plan; I am saying the individual must have a general plan. Many of the spontaneous things that happened in the Bible happened as people worked a plan. Peter and John did not just decide to go pray; they were working their plan. On the way to work their plan, something spontaneous happened. So it is with all the major events of the Bible. God gives a plan and seemingly spontaneous events occur along the way.

Even Jesus sent out a pre-crusade team to prepare the people to receive ministry. We erroneously get the idea that He just spontaneously made every decision and the crowds thronged him. Luke 10:1 says, *"After these things the Lord appointed other seventy also, and sent them two by two before his face into every city and place, where he himself would come."* He sent workers to prepare the people to receive ministry.

The early church had a two-fold plan of action; they ministered publicly in the temple as well as privately from house to house. *"And daily in the temple, and in every house, they ceased not to teach and preach Jesus Christ.*" Acts 5:42. The early church had its first great moves publicly. But later, house to house became the most effective method. One must never marry a method. Whatever will work for you in your area is the way you should do it. But in other cultures, different methods may need to be discovered.

One of my most effective leadership seminars is "Relevant Ministry." In this seminar we teach leaders how to get in touch with the needs of their community. Recognizing those needs is the beginning of developing a plan.

The main complaint against the church is that it is not relevant. Unfortunately, this is a legitimate complaint. We tend to formulate plans within the walls of the church. We fail to ask questions and respond accordingly. We vary our methods with little concern for what will be effective with the people.

If you do not have a plan or the confidence for personal ministry, simply take them to church. When they go to church, they will hear the gospel. They will meet many wonderful people. Most importantly, they should have a personal encounter with Jesus. By being in a worship service they will experience the presence of God. The presence of God can do more to soften a hard heart than our words can ever do.

Ironically, many Christians are hesitant about bringing people to church. They are afraid of how the visitor will react. We are often afraid of how they will view praise and worship. Do not try to second-guess anybody. Let God and them work it out.

The first great evangelistic thrust in the New Testament church came as the believers worshipped God unashamedly. "*And when the day of Pentecost was fully come, they were all with one accord in one place. And suddenly there came a sound from heaven like a rushing mighty wind, and it filled all the house where they were sitting. And there appeared unto them cloven tongues like as of fire, and it sat upon each of them. And they were all filled with the Holy Ghost, and began to speak with other tongues, as the Spirit gave them utterance."* Acts 2:1-4. The result of this bold, public worship was three thousand new converts.

We need not be apologetic for the gifts of the Holy Spirit or free worship and praise. The world is looking for something that is worth believing in. But most Christians are so apologetic about spiritual things that the world does not want what they have.

Do not be afraid to worship freely in front of your friends. Do not put on a show, but do not be ashamed. Show them who it is that is transforming your life. In other words, DO NOT BE ASHAMED OF JESUS. On the day of Pentecost, the believers were not in the upper room as some suppose. They were staying in the upper room, but they went to the temple for prayer and worship. They were in the midst of unbelievers when they began to worship in other tongues.

But, you might say, the Bible says unbelievers will think you are crazy if you worship in tongues in front of them. That is true, but not detrimental. 1 Corinthians 14:23 says, *"If, therefore, the whole church be come together into one place, and all speak with tongues, and there come in those that are un-learned, or unbelievers, will they not say that ye are mad?"* This scripture is not opposing worshipping in tongues; however, it is explaining how the ignorant and unbelieving will react to tongues. That reaction was what provided the opportunity to win 3000 on the day of Pentecost. Likewise, it will give you opportunity to minister to those who respond ignorantly through criticism.

Every instance in the Book of Acts where people were baptized in the Holy Spirit, they all worshipped in tongues at one time and no one interpreted. Everyone worshipping in tongues together is not out of order, unruly or a bad witness. On the day of Pentecost the early church worshipped in other tongues. Some did accuse them of being drunk, just as some will accuse you of being crazy. But this simply reveals the condition of their hearts and opens the door for ministry.

Anytime one forbids or criticizes worshipping in the Spirit in public, we are to respond as Peter did. Rather than apologize and feel intimidated, we are to seize this as an opportunity to minister to their need. *"But Peter, standing up with the eleven, lifted up his voice, and said unto them, Ye men of Judaea, and all ye that dwell at Jerusalem, be this known unto you, and hearken to my words; For these are not drunken, as ye suppose, seeing it is but the third hour of the day."* Acts 2:14-15. Peter saw their ignorance and criticism as an opportunity to minister to their need.

When someone criticizes worship and the gifts, the Scripture identifies them as either ignorant or unbelieving. I cannot let the ignorance or unbelief of another dictate my theology or relationship with Jesus. I must see this as a need and respond with understanding, kindness and ministry.

Lost and needy people need to see and experience the power of God moving in a worship service. If their hearts are hard, it will be revealed; if not, they will receive. I have noticed that many times when a believer brings someone to church, they become very reserved in their worship and praise. Do not fall prey to that intimidation. You do not need to put on a show for them, but you do need to express your freedom and joy in the Lord.

As people become interested in what you have, take them to the place where you receive. Until you become capable of leading others to the Lord, this is a wonderful way to start. Even after you win people to Jesus, you should always seek to get them involved in church with you. By going to church with you, you will be able to encourage them and help them grow. You will also provide them with a sense of accountability and community.

Of course, this means that you need to attend a church where you feel comfortable bringing friends. A lack of confidence in your church will be a great deterrent to personal ministry.[1]

About every four months, our church has a special service we call "Soul Saving Sunday." Everything about this service is designed to make the lost and hurting feel safe and comfortable.

There is a momentum in group ministry that is sometimes missing in personal ministry. Often times, those who are unresponsive in a one-on-one setting are

---

[1] *"My Church My Family: How to Have a Healthy Relationship with the Church"* is a very crucial book for understanding how to have a healthy relationship with a church. It also helps one understand how to select a church.

very receptive in a group.

17

House to House

"And daily in the temple, and in every house, they ceased not to teach and preach Jesus Christ." Acts 5:42. Besides what happened in the public meetings, the early church was active house to house. They met in people's homes to teach, preach and fellowship. House to house ministry is any ministry you take to the people. I am convinced this is the most powerful approach to reaching and developing people.

The church is commanded to go out where the people are. Instead, we have tried to get them to come to where we are. As mentioned earlier, there are some who will come to us; however, the majority will have to be won "on their own turf."

One of the requirements for ministers is hospitality. 1 Timothy 3:2 says, *"A bishop then must be... given to hospitality, apt to teach."* The ability to deal with people one-on-one is essential for effective ministry. The early believers opened their homes to reach family, neighbors and friends. The home created a non-threatening, safe environment that made ministry natural and easy.

Some of the greatest sermons and meetings in the Bible took place one-on-one or in very small groups. This is where effective ministry takes place. In America we have developed a false sense of success. We all want to stand in front of the large crowds and have our own ministries. That gratifies the ego, but it is not what builds strong Christians. The ones who make a commitment and see it through are the ones who have a close personal tie with another believer. We must remember that the masses all received ministry one at a time.

I have started churches across my kitchen table. As I have moved into new areas, taken new jobs or met new people, I began to witness and invite them into my home. Several different times, through personal ministry, I have had home groups of thirty or more people. These were people I could not get to come to church, but they would come to my house. As these people became stable, I either started churches or put them in churches.

When your home becomes a refuge of ministry, it effects your entire family. Your children and mate become involved in ministry. It is no longer something you do that takes you away from your family; it becomes something you do that involves your family. They get to see the results of personal ministry.

My children grew up seeing people get saved, healed and delivered in our dining room. They prayed with us as we ministered to hurting people. Ministry was not something done in the back room at church; it was a way of life. My children have led dozens of people to Jesus because it has never been foreign to them. Our home has been a place of prayer and ministry.

Daily ministry is a part of the lifestyle ministry

we spoke of in another chapter. Lifestyle ministry is far more demanding than ministry in the traditional sense because it does demand a change in your entire lifestyle. But this is by far the most effective ministry there is. This type of ministry affects who we are and how we live our life.

Dr. Cho teaches about the power of the homogeneous cell group. Because people feel comfortable with a group of peers, the trust level is higher. People who are won through a peer are far more likely to attend church and follow through on their commitment. Your house is the most holy place to bring a person for ministry.

Most people dread and fear the idea of "going out witnessing." We have all been harassed by the Jehovah's Witness, and we know how badly we dread seeing them come to our house. We have heard the horror stories about confrontations on the street, so invariably we never go.

Rather than going out on the street, it would be far better to seize the opportunities that surround you in day-to-day life. Colossians 4:5-6 says, *"Walk in wisdom toward them that are without, redeeming the time. Let your speech be always with grace, seasoned with salt, that ye may know how ye ought to answer every man."* The New International Version translates "redeeming the time" as making the most of every opportunity.

Our dilemma is not a lack of people to minister to, but our great lack is in seizing the opportunities. As I mentioned before, every fault a person has is an opportunity. Nearly every conversation creates some opportunity. The self-absorbed person does not really listen when others talk. He is preparing his next statement. Therefore, he is unaware of the needs others express. Let's examine some ways to create and seize those opportunities without being pushy or negative.

Make a part of your daily prayer a time of preparation. Ask the Lord to make you more aware of the needs and opportunities that surround you. Keep in mind that this Scripture, as well as the one quoted from Peter, speaks of us giving people an answer, which means they ask us questions. Live a life of salt. Salt makes a person thirsty. Live a life that makes people ask questions. Prepare your heart daily for ministry.

While attending Bible College I began to "dry up." I went to school with Christians, and I worked with Christians. I was surrounded by Christians. I never had opportunity to witness to the lost. I knew witnessing was a part of my natural walk with God. I was getting dissatisfied and knew the reason--a failure to give life.

Before going to bed one night I prayed, "Lord, if you do not send me some people to witness to, I am leaving this place." The next morning on my way to work I had the most unusual experience. As I sat at a traffic light at six in the morning, I heard a tapping sound at my window. When I looked up, I saw a man knocking on my car window. In desperation he begged, "I saw your bumper sticker; if you will, pull over and tell me how to get saved."

I pulled over, ministered to him and we prayed together for Jesus to come into his life. My enthusiasm from that experience made me go to work with a different attitude every day. I began looking for and expecting opportunities to minister. I found that I had been surrounded by opportunity all along, but I had failed to seize those opportunities.

Do not be a nuisance when ministering; be an example. Never "talk at" people; talk TO them. When they talk about their interests, LISTEN! A great communicator is always a great listener. Never condemn them or their actions. Condemning always makes the other person defensive and non-responsive. When you listen, they believe you care.

Be assumptive. I always talk to people as if I assume they believe just like I do. With this approach, even those that do not believe will often act as if they do. The assumptive approach makes a person feel accepted. You are not challenging them; you are simply conducting a conversation.

When witnessing to my family members, I always assumed they wanted to hear what I had to say. I would talk about how good God was. I would talk about Him answering prayer. They would talk back to me comfortably because they thought I really did think they were "right" with the Lord. It soon became very comfortable for us to talk about the things of God.

I heard a statement a few years ago that has really stuck with me. "Those who will influence your life the most are not the ones you believe in, but the ones who believe in you."[1] There is so much truth to this. The assumptive approach always conveys a belief in the other person. When they see you are not preaching at them, but sharing with them, they are totally disarmed.

To be effective in any area of ministry, it is

---

[1] Source Unknown.

essential that you have value for those you desire to reach. This cannot be "fake." If it is, they will know it right away.

Work has always been a great mission field for me. I did not stop working to witness to people, that would have been unfair to my employer. But as we worked and "shot the breeze," I would talk about the Lord and how good and merciful and kind He is. By being assumptive, I always presented the gospel in a positive way.

On one particular job I was a "B operator," which meant I had to assist the "A operators." There was one "A operator" who always gave me the dirtiest, hardest work. I would maintain a good attitude, and at every opportunity, I would talk about the Lord. Over a year after I left that job, I received a call from that particular operator. He had gotten saved. He told me how he had deliberately given me jobs to get me away from him. My talking about the Lord always got him under conviction. Yet after all that time, he was unable to "shake" that conviction. One night on the side of the road he did what he had heard me talk about. He prayed the sinner's prayer and became a new creation.

Many times I would go into work and share the testimonies of people I had led to the Lord. I would tell every detail. I would always act as if I thought these guys were saved, so they never felt threatened. I would tell the "sinner's prayer" word for word. I wanted to make sure they would know what to do when they were ready to get saved.

On that particular job, several people were saved. One man is now in the ministry as a result of my casual, assumptive conversations with my fellow

workers. Work was always a joy because of the opportunities it presented to minister. Where else could I be
paid to spend time with sinners and they could not
leave?

This is the kind of ministry that reaches and
keeps people. You have more influence over the people
that know you personally than anyone else. Your family and friends are your mission field. Your positive,
open approach to sharing the gospel with them is more
powerful than all the sermons they could ever hear.

We have mistakenly assumed that the apostles
preaching sermons did the great evangelism in the
book of Acts. The first great conversions took place as
the apostles preached, but that mentality almost killed
the early church. They saw a few thousand people get
saved at Pentecost and at the temple gate and fell into a
"preacher/laymen" mentality. This was a natural carry
over from the Old Testament priesthood.

The early church did not obey the commission
of Jesus to reach the world. They settled down in
Jerusalem and had church. It was not until the persecution in Acts 8 that the gospel was carried to the world.
Acts 8:1 & 4 gives an account of the persecution: "*And
Saul was consenting unto his death. And at that time
there was a great persecution against the church which
was at Jerusalem; and they were all scattered abroad
throughout the regions of Judaea and Samaria, except
the apostles. Therefore, they that were scattered
abroad went everywhere preaching the word.*" They
did not preach to the world because of this great
compassion for the lost. They went to the world to
avoid persecution.

It is noteworthy that the apostles did not scatter

with them. If the apostles had gone, the Word would have probably been restricted. The apostles did not believe the Samaritans could have the same experience as themselves. It was not a preacher that won Samaria; it was a believer in someone's home.

In Acts 9, the apostles could not believe Saul was actually born again. God did not send him to an apostle to receive ministry; He sent him to a believer called Ananias. The apostles would have made a mess out of Paul for sure. They would have probably considered his loss of sight as judgement from God and gloated over his plight. This compassionate "layman" got Paul saved and healed.

In Acts 10, God had to move on a Gentile proselyte in order for the Gentiles to be saved. "Surely the Gentiles could not have what the Jews had." God had to send them to find someone to preach the gospel to them. Only after God had visited Peter and sent the men out to find them, would he "stoop" to preaching to Gentiles. Even then he had to defend his actions before the other apostles.

The gospel was then spread to the other Gentiles as a result of Cornelius gathering them together in his house, not because Peter carried the Word. Because the Gentiles were being reached, the total center of Christian activities shifted from Jerusalem to Antioch in Acts 13. Antioch became the church that was reaching the world, not Jerusalem.

Acts 19 shows that Paul did not reach all of Asia. He taught daily in the school of Tyrannus. It was the people who heard him teach that carried the Word to all of Asia. *"But when divers were hardened, and believed not, but spake evil of that way before the multitude, he departed from them, and separated the disciples, disputing daily in the school of one, Tyrannus. And this continued for the space of two years; so that all they who dwelt in Asia heard the word of the Lord Jesus, both Jews and Greeks."* Acts 19:9-10.

As powerful as public preaching may be, it will never replace the effectiveness of one-on-one. I love all forms of outreach. I participate in crusades, radio and television. But I never fool myself into thinking these will be the tools that will reach the masses. These will be tools that strengthen, train and encourage the believers as they reach the masses daily, house-to-house.

The rise of church buildings came simultaneously with the fall of true spirituality. Church buildings are not evil. Yet, what they represent has been a part of something very evil, crippling and disempowering.

Use buildings as tools, but let your home be a place of life and ministry. Turn your house into a real sanctuary. Make your kitchen table an altar for the Lord and minister to your part of the world.

18

The Power of Spoken Words

One of the greatest fears of personal ministry stems from a lack of confidence in the Word of God. We fail to understand what happens when people believe the Word. We think it will be our technique, skill or personal persuasion that will convince them to receive ministry.

The truth is, our skill and technique may open doors for us, but only the Word of God spoken in love will melt a cold, hard heart. For too long we have been dependent on the carnality of man to present the gospel - so much so that the Gospel has been robbed of its power. Paul made it clear in 1 Corinthians 1:17 that he did not depend on the wisdom of man, *"For Christ sent me not to baptize but to preach the Gospel; not with wisdom of words, lest the cross of Christ should be made of none effect."*

Several years ago, I was training teams for street ministry. There was one man who could never memorize any of the material. He had difficulty even pronouncing the words properly, but he had a desire to win the lost. He would go out on the streets, stop people and read the tract to them, word-for-word. Keep in mind, he could not read that well. Every time he went out, people were saved. He had no style, but he did have truth. As he spoke the truth and people believed, dozens were saved.

The Lord does not confirm people, He confirms the Word. Mark 16:20 says, "*And they went forth, and preached everywhere, the Lord working with them, and confirming the Word with signs following. Amen.*" The Lord confirmed the Word they spoke. He did not confirm their skills. He did not confirm their call. The word "them" is not actually in the original text. So it should read, "...the Lord worked with and confirmed the Word..."

When we speak the Word, the Lord has something to work with. Winning the lost does not depend solely on our communication skills or personal abilities. As a matter of fact, the person who has the greatest skills will usually get the least long-term results. Someone who has the "gift of gab" will often fail to depend on the Lord. They will usually not even depend on the Word; they will depend on their power of persuasion. Persuasion produces temporary results, but when the new wears off, those people will only be affected in their emotions. They will not be affected in their hearts, unless their confidence and hope is in the Word.

I always have a difficult time training preachers, salesmen and outgoing people. They lean so heavily on their personal skills that it is difficult for them to trust God. Some of the greatest soul winners I have ever trained had very poor communication skills. One night a man walked up to me and mumbled, "I wanna learn to win the lost." I could not even understand him. I said, "What did you say?" "I wanna learn to win souls," he repeated. He would never look me in the eye. He was wearing blue jeans, black boots, a black leather jacket and a hairstyle that was twenty years out of date.

I committed to take him out one time. I told him what to do to prepare and told him what day we would go out. When the day came, he was ready-- fearful and nervous, but ready. Because he did not have the confidence to do his own thing, he did it exactly the way I taught. From the first day, he became the most effective soul winner I had ever trained. When he went out, he worked the plan, used the scripture, trusted God and won the lost. Because he had no confidence in his own abilities, he had no choice other than depending on the Word of God. He spoke the Word and God worked with it and confirmed it.

If we will ever understand the power of God's Word, our confidence will be in the Word, not ourselves. Luke 1:37, *"For with God nothing shall be impossible."* The ASV translates accordingly, *"For no Word of God shall be void of power."* God's Word has power when mixed with faith. (Hebrews 4:2). When it is spoken, the Holy Spirit has something with which to work. They may reject it or accept it, but the results are no longer up to us. After I have delivered the Word in love, the rest is up to the Spirit and the individual.

Conviction is the work of the Holy Spirit. It is not our job to manipulate their emotions to get results. The Spirit reproves (convinces) the world of sin, and of righteousness, and of judgment according to John 16:8.

He does convincing with the Word we speak. If we play on their emotions, their decisions will waiver according to their emotions. 2 Corinthians 7:10 says it this way, *"For godly sorrow worketh repentance to salvation not to be repented of; but the sorrow of the world worketh death."*

It is all right for someone's emotions to be affected by love and truth. In fact, the truth should affect our emotions. We are told to believe in our heart, and our heart is the seat of emotions. Therefore, real believing always affects the emotions. Perhaps I should show the distinction between an emotional experience and a spiritual experience. An emotional experience is when something simply affects our emotions, independent of truth. A spiritual experience, on the other hand, is when truth, or the Spirit of God, deals with us in such a way that it effects our emotions. The latter will set you free. The former will deceive you. The emotions will always be effected. They question is, however, are they effected by truth.

When I surrendered my life to the Lord, I heard one scripture quoted, mingled with cursing and swearing. Until that time, no one had ever spoken scripture to me. I had been told I would go to hell. I had even been told God loved me, but no one ever spoke scripture to me. Matthew 12:30 was the scripture he quoted, *"He that is not with me is against me; and he that gathereth not with me scattereth abroad."*

When I heard that scripture, the Holy Spirit had something to work with. My heart was "cut to the quick." My emotions were touched with the conviction of the Holy Spirit. The Word of God became a two-edged sword that cut through my defense mechanisms. There are no arguments for the voice of the Lord in your heart.

Hebrews 4:12 says, "For the word of God is quick, alive, and powerful, and sharper than any two edged sword, piercing even to the dividing asunder of soul and spirit, and of the joints and marrow, and is a discerner of the thoughts and intents of the heart." When the living Word gets in us, it can separate our thoughts and intentions.

Jesus said in John 6:63, *"It is the Spirit that quickeneth; the flesh profiteth nothing. The Words that I speak unto you, they are Spirit, and they are life."* Because the Word of God is Spirit and life, it can produce spiritual fruit. The flesh can make you feel guilty, sad or glad, but only the Spirit can give life.

Trust in the power of the Word of God. You are not limited to your abilities. In fact, if you trust in them, your abilities will be what limits your productivity. 1 Corinthians 4:20 says, *"For the kingdom of God is not in word, but in power."* My words and abilities have no power. Yet, when I speak His Word, the power of Almighty God goes to work.

Because I trust in the Word, I am also able to stop talking. After speaking the Word of God I can wait confidently as the Spirit of God goes to work. If I do not trust the Word, I will feel compelled to chatter on, trying to convince the hearer. Many times it is our endless chatter that gets in the way of the Holy Spirit.

So many times after sharing the Word, I have simply leaned back and waited. I cannot tell you how many times I sat and stared at the person waiting on a response. Everything in me wanted to start talking and explaining. The silence seemed like eternity, but as I waited, the Holy Spirit worked. Many times, after a long silence, a tear would roll down their cheek. They would break in the presence of the Lord. In my silence, God was able to speak.

Early in my ministry, I wanted to know how Jesus got the particular results He did. I would get frustrated when I would try to figure out exactly what He said to His followers. I could see He was getting results, but I did not know what He said to get those results.

I began to notice the phrase "Gospel of the Kingdom." This was Jesus' message. The word "gospel," simply defined means "good news." Jesus always had good news for the poor, sick, broken-hearted, demon possessed and sinful. Good news for these people was not a verbal beating. It was not a message that explained why they were in the condition they were in. Good news was the message of deliverance and freedom from their condition.

God finally spoke to my heart and said, "If it is not good news, it is not GOSPEL." Every time I would prepare a message, I would hear this question, "Is that going to be good news for the hearers." I would often have to admit, "If I were in need, hearing this message would not be good news for me."

If I want Jesus' results, I must use His method. He always had good news for the people. When we preach the Word, it should set people free, not make them bound. The Word should heal the hurting, not finish them off. We should love those in need, not hate them.

When we speak the Word, we should always check our motive. If we are trying to "straighten out," prove we are right or any motive other than love, we are not going to get good results. Proverbs says, "*A word fitly spoken is like apples of gold in pictures of silver.*" Proverbs 25:11. The way we present the Gospel should be attractive. We should make learning a joy. We should develop our communication skills, yet our trust should be in God and His Word.

When people detect love and sincerity, they will open their hearts to your message. If they sense haughtiness, condemnation or a condescending attitude, they will resist you. So speak the truth in love, and the results will be phenomenal. If you minister in love and speak the truth, you have a situation conducive to ministry. You need not depend on showmanship or style, because the truth will be unhindered. As one man once said, "If I do not take the credit when things go right, I do not have to take the blame when they go wrong." Not only will the Word be unhindered, you will be out from under the pressure.

When the Holy Spirit convicts, He never condemns. He never points to the problem; He always points to the solution. The guilt that people feel about their sin is simply their own conscience. When we see God's solutions, it is hard not to feel guilty. Yet, it is not God's work to make a person feel guilty.

If we are to work with Him, it is important that our words also point to the solutions and clarify the promises. We want to make the path straight, not crooked. We want to minister the words of life.

19

The Message
of Reconciliation

Every Christian is called to be a minister of the Gospel (good news) of Jesus Christ. More specifically, we are to be witnesses. A witness is a person who has first-hand knowledge of the facts. As Christians, we are witnesses to the fact that Jesus has risen from the dead and that he has forgiven our sins. This is called the "Ministry of Reconciliation."

In 2 Corinthians 5:19, Paul clearly states what the message of reconciliation is: *"that God was reconciling the world to Himself in Christ, not counting men's sins against them..."* (NIV) This is the Good News: God has already forgiven men's sins. Christ died and carried the sins of the entire world. Not only did he take the sins of the entire world, but He also took the punishment for all those sins. I Timothy 4:10 says, *"...we have put our hope in the living God, who is the Savior of all men, and especially those who believe."* (NIV) Jesus did not die for the sins of a few; He died for the sins of all men. God, through Jesus Christ, was reconciling all men of all ages to Himself. He has already done away with the sins of all men. An individual must believe and confess Jesus as Lord before this will be of any value to him, but the point is this: God has already forgiven all men's sins.

This is the message we should carry to the world: God has already forgiven your sins. He did it when Jesus died on the cross. What great news this is to the person who is struggling with sin and guilt. It is no longer a question of God being willing to forgive-- because he has already forgiven.

Many times when I am out on the streets, I will give a person a tract and make a statement like; "Did you know that God is not mad at you?" Most of the time the person looks totally shocked. You see, most people think God is angry at the world. They think He is just waiting for the chance to punish them for their sin. Those who want to get saved are usually wondering if God is willing. Many times I have had people say, "I am afraid that I may have done too much, God may not be willing to forgive me." But the Good News is that God has already forgiven. Do you want to receive and experience this free gift? This brings such relief to so many people.

People remain in bondage primarily because of fear. Most sinners have a fear of judgement. All they have ever heard about God was that He was going to judge the world. That fear will often lead to arrogance, defiance or even hatred of God. They get tough on the outside because on the inside they are afraid and ashamed of their guilt. You see, according to 1 John 4:18, "...*fear has to do with punishment*..." (NIV) If you think God is trying to punish you, there is no alternative but to resist Him.

Hebrews teaches us that fear is the power which

holds people captive. *"And deliver them who, through fear of death, were all their lifetime subject to bondage."* Hebrews 2:15. The church has taught that fear would get people saved, but the Bible presents something entirely different. Hell will be full of people who were controlled by their fears. *"But the fearful, and unbelieving, and the abominable, and murderers, and whoremongers, and sorcerers, and idolaters, and all liars, shall have their part in the lake which burneth with fire and brimstone: which is the second death."* Revelation 21:8.

I believe the fear that Satan uses to control and manipulate is the fear of punishment of our sins. That fear causes us to enter into deceit, self-righteousness, blame shifting and all manner of evil. Love, on the other hand, gives us the freedom to be honest and repentive. Fear breeds deception; love breeds honesty. Fear breeds unbelief, love breeds faith.

The awareness of the love of God will set a person free from fear. 1 John 4:18a says, *"There is no fear in love. But perfect love drives out fear..."* When a sinner hears the Good News of God's love, the fear in his heart will be driven out. When he discovers and believes that his sins are already forgiven and he is not required to beg and persuade God to answer his prayers, he will be set free from bondage.

Understand, no one will go to hell because of his sins. If this were the case, we would relate to God on the basis of works and there would have been no reason for Jesus to come to the earth and die. Jesus died for our sins. We must believe on His finished work (that God raised Him from the dead) and confess Him as Lord of our life. A person will, therefore, be sent to hell, not because his sins were not forgiven, but because he refused the free gift of righteousness in Jesus.

Romans 10:9 says, *"That if you CONFESS WITH YOUR MOUTH Jesus is Lord and believe in your heart that God raised him from the dead, YOU WILL BE SAVED."* (NIV). If Jesus did away with your sins, you do not have to carry the punishment for them. If Jesus actually rose from the dead, then you have eternal life through Him. Therefore, when you believe this in your heart, you are justified (made righteous). *"For it is with your heart that you believe and are justified."* Romans 10:10 (NIV).

When you believe God raised Him from the dead, you are relieved from the guilt. There is no guilt when sins have been paid for. After believing the truth of the Good News, the next step is confession. Since Jesus did all of this to set me free from sin and its penalties, He is worthy to be Lord (boss) of my life. Therefore, one must confess with his mouth that Jesus is Lord. The Bible says, *"It is with your mouth that you confess and are saved."* Romans 10:10 (NIV).

For years we have been taught that a sinner must confess his sins to be saved. The truth is, it would take years to confess all our sins. There are things we have done that we do not realize. Do you confess the "big" ones and forget the "little" ones? NO! Confessing our sins does not get us saved. Confessing Jesus Christ as Lord of our lives gets us saved. The word "confess" means to "say the same thing." In other words, our words must reflect what is in our hearts. There is no magic in saying the words. The "magic" is when those words reflect a belief of the heart.

Only when we have understood the message of reconciliation are we able to go out to the world with an attitude and a message that really gives life. Only then do we have the good news they need to hear.

The message of reconciliation tells us that God did all we would ever need through Jesus. He became our sin so we would not have to stay sinners. He took the curse of the law so we would never be punished for our sins. He went to hell so we would never have to pay the ultimate price for our sins. He conquered our sins when He arose from the dead so we would never need to fight the battle with our sin. He obtained our righteousness so we would never have to earn it. He gives it to us as a free gift, thereby, qualifying us for all of the promises of God. In so doing, He is worthy to be our Lord.

This is the good news the world needs to hear. When we believe and accept the finished work of Jesus, the grace of God empowers us to experience the life of God.

20

Witnessing One-on-One

In this section we will move on to some practical tips in ministering to people one-on-one. I want to start with street witnessing. The main thing that is different about street witnessing is the approach. Regardless of what type of witnessing you are doing, it will all be the same once you get down to leading someone to the Lord. Only the initial approach will be different.

When dealing with family, friends or fellow employees, you will be more conversational and tactful. But keep in mind, when you get to the place where you are ready to get them saved it will be the same. That is when you share what I call "Creation to Calvary."

When going out on the streets, one should have a clear-cut plan. Many people do not like to work from a plan, but I have found that results are always better when I have a plan and STICK TO IT. If the Holy Spirit wants to change my plan, He is more than welcome, but until he does, I stick to a clear-cut plan of action. My plan in a nutshell is this: First, I like to use tracts. Tracts are good icebreakers. If you have a tract, then you always have a non-threatening way to approach a person.

Next, I am going to explain what I call "Creation to Calvary." Then I am going to explain Romans 10:9, and last of all I am going to lead them in a sinners' prayer. If they will not pray the sinner's prayer, then I am going to shift to my second objective.

If I cannot get them saved, I will make sure they know how to get saved. Many times after I have witnessed to someone who has initially rejected the gospel, they were later saved because the plan was so clearly explained.

All of this can be done in 5 to 10 minutes. When ministering on the street, I have found that if you beat around the bush, stall or take too long, you make the person suspicious and uneasy. It is essential to get down to business.

The following is almost word for word how I approach a sinner on the street:

Witness: You wouldn't mind reading something about the Lord would you? (Ask that question in a very assumptive tone of voice. They assume you will give them something to read and leave them alone.)

Sinner: I guess not.

Witness: I am doing this to let people know that God loves you, Jesus died for you, and I care about you. (This is on the front of the tract. Point to this as you make the statements)

Sinner: Yes, well thanks.

Witness: Can I take just a minute and show you
           something?

Sinner: Well, I am in a hurry.

Witness: That's o.k. It will only take a minute. I
           will walk along with you. Did you know
           that God put man here to love? Man was
           placed on the earth in a garden called Eden.
           It was a paradise. God never desired that
           the world be like it is today. I am sure you
           have heard about Adam and Eve in the
           garden and how they sinned.

Sinner: No, I haven't.

Witness: Really? Well, that is what happened. Now,
           since God is a holy God, He has to judge
           sin. But, since God put man here to love,
           He does not want to judge him. Let me
           show you how much God loves you. In
           order to keep from punishing you, He sent
           His son Jesus into the world. At the end of
           His life, He was crucified. While hanging
           on the cross, God poured all the sins that
           the world would ever commit on Him.
           Jesus took all the sin and the punishment
           for sin. That means every sin you have
           ever committed, as well as any sin you will
           ever commit, Jesus has already taken the
           punishment for you. God loved you so
           much that instead of punishing you for
           your sins, He let Jesus take the punish-
           ment. After Jesus died, God raised Him

from the dead, and He overcame death. God desires to give us all that Jesus received at the Resurrection. All God asks of us is this: to believe that God raised Jesus from the dead and confess him as our Lord. Do you believe that God raised Jesus from the dead?

Sinner: I don't know.

Witness: Are you willing to believe?

Sinner: I guess.

Witness: Since you are willing to take God at his Word and believe that he raised Jesus from the dead, you are halfway there. Look at this verse. Romans 10:9 says, "*If you confess with your mouth Jesus as Lord and believe in your heart that God raised Jesus from the dead, you will be saved.*" (NIV) Now, you have already said that you believe God raised Jesus from the dead, so all you have to do is confess him as Lord, and you will be saved. All of your past will be forgiven, all of your past will be behind you, and you can start life over as a new person free from sin. Would you like that?

Sinner: Sure I would.

Witness: Well, the Bible says if you confess with your mouth Jesus as Lord and believe in your heart that God raised him from the dead you will be saved. Since you already believe that God raised Jesus from the dead, is there any reason why you could not confess him as Lord? (This is the first question that calls for a negative answer. If he has any objections, just listen until he gets through. Answer those objections and then proceed. I usually minimize the objection with something like this. "I know these are all legitimate problems, but they are not worth giving up eternal life for, are they?")

Witness: Would you like to pray or would you rather me lead you in a prayer? (Very assumptive.)

Sinner: (Looks around as if he might be embarrassed) I don't know.

Witness: That's all right, I am not going to embarrass you. I pray with people in public all the time. This will only take a minute, and it is a decision that you have to make. Would you rather pray, or would you like for me to lead you in a prayer?

Sinner: You lead me in a prayer.

Witness: All right, as I lead you, you pray out loud to God. The Bible says you have to say it with your mouth. You are not praying to me. You are praying to God, who will hear you and do just what His Word says He will do. All right, "Father, I believe that you raised Jesus from the dead. I believe that He died for my sins. Because He died for my sins, I confess Him as Lord of my life. Jesus, you are now my Lord, my boss. I give you my life. I am going to live for you...come into my life...make me a new person...change me...cleanse me from my sin. Thank you for saving me...Amen..."

After that, I do a little follow-up, such as getting their name, address and phone number.

I have used this approach for several years and have had great success with it. "Creation to Calvary" clears up many of the misconceptions people have about God. Romans 10:9 tells them what to do now that they know the truth, and the Spirit of God takes care of the rest.

Let me encourage you to memorize this approach and do just as I have done it here. Discipline yourself to use a proven method before you try to develop your own technique. Practice it on a friend, say it out loud in the car when you are by yourself, and then go out and put it into practice. Many people simply read the tract until they have it memorized.

When "street witnessing" pick a place where people do not seem to be in a hurry: parks, parking lots (those who are waiting in cars), shopping centers (those that are sitting on benches or that seem to be killing time). Then do it JUST LIKE IT IS WRITTEN. If you approach a person who is in a hurry you will usually be an annoyance. People in a hurry usually have somewhere they need to be. Those who are not, tend to be more open and receptive.

If a person does not want to get saved at that

moment, make sure they know the two things they must do to get saved. Many times we have people turn us down in public only to make a commitment later.

While driving back from a meeting one night, I stopped to get a soft drink. I began to share "Creation to Calvary" with the sales clerk. There was no one in the store, and I was not interfering with her work. When I tried to lead her in the prayer, she would not pray. I talked to her and made sure she understood the two things she had to do to be saved. I even had her repeat them to me.

I gave her my phone number and told her to call me when she had made a decision. The next day the call came. She had surrendered her life to Jesus. The reason she would not pray with me the night before was embarrassment. She had never prayed aloud in her entire life.

When people turn you down, do not become defensive or argumentative. Stay assumptive and walk in love. Once you give them the Word, the Holy Spirit never stops dealing with them. Do not consider a postponement as a failure. If they know what to do they may do it in the future. I have had people call me years after hearing the salvation message.

Once you have shared the Word, your job is done. You have no control over results. You only have control over how clearly you share the Word.

"Creation to Calvary" tracts, as well as follow-up cards, are available through Impact International Publications. See back page for complete details and ordering information.

21

Ministering the Baptism in the Holy Spirit

The baptism in the Holy Spirit is essential for every believer. Whenever possible, we lead people into the baptism of the Holy Spirit immediately. In America, this is a little more difficult than overseas. In other countries, we will get people saved on the streets and often times lead them into the baptism in the Holy Spirit immediately. It is wonderful to see these brand new converts worshipping God in other tongues within a few minutes after they have been born again. This is the pattern found in the Book of Acts.

In America, it is more difficult to minister in this area because people have been conditioned against the truth. Church History[1] shows that all the early church spoke in tongues. It was not until Christianity tried to be made socially acceptable that the baptism in the Holy Spirit and speaking in other tongues was diminished.

In Acts chapter eight, the apostles went imme-

---

[1] Larry Lea, "*Mending the Nets & Broken Fishermen,*" Church on the Rock, Rockwell, Texas

diately to Samaria to minister the baptism in the Holy Spirit when they realized the people had not yet received. *"Now when the apostles who were at Jerusalem heard that Samaria had received the word of God, they sent unto them Peter and John, Who, when they were come down, prayed for them, that they might receive the Holy Ghost; For as yet he was fallen upon none of them; only they were baptized in the name of the Lord Jesus. Then laid they their hands on them, and they received the Holy Ghost."* Acts 8: 14-17.

They knew the standard procedure was for all believers to receive the baptism in the Holy Spirit. They saw it as an essential part of following the Lord Jesus. He had promised this wonderful gift to all believers.

In Acts chapter ten, there was no great time lapse. The Gentiles believed, were born again and immediately were baptized in the Holy Spirit. *"While Peter yet spoke these words, the Holy Ghost fell on all them who heard the word. And they of the circumcision who believed were astonished, as many as came with Peter, because on the Gentiles also was poured out the gift of the Holy Ghost. For they heard them speak with tongues, and magnify God. Then answered Peter, Can any man forbid water, that these should not be baptized, who have received the Holy Ghost as well as we?"* Acts 10:44-47.

We see this again in the nineteenth chapter. *"When they heard this, they were baptized in the name of the Lord Jesus. And when Paul had laid his hands upon them, the Holy Ghost came on them, and they spake with tongues, and prophesied."* Acts 19:5-6.

Immediately after they were born again, Paul baptized these new converts in water and led them into the baptism in the Holy Spirit.

The scriptural pattern is to follow through with the baptism in the Holy Spirit as a part of evangelism. Keep in mind, we are to undo all the works of the devil and thoroughly equip every new believer. Anything Jesus died to give is available to all. If it will bring victory to their lives, minister it to them.

Since everything is received by faith, we must build faith in the new believer. Sharing scriptures about the promise of the new birth builds faith to be born again. Likewise, sharing scriptures about the baptism in the Holy Spirit builds faith to receive this area of ministry.

Do not be afraid to share the baptism in the Holy Spirit. However, in this country, it would be inappropriate to share it on the streets except for rare occasions. The goal is for the person to receive. They cannot receive what they do not believe or desire. An attempt to minister anything to a person in an environment that produces embarrassment will decrease the possibility of success. Never attempt to minister until a person expresses belief. If they do not believe, they cannot receive.

When you feel it is appropriate, begin to share and build faith. The number one hindrance to people receiving will be the way we share it. If we share it reluctantly or with hesitance, they will be reluctant and hesitant to receive. If we share it in love with confidence, that is the way they will receive.

The following is a brief synopsis of how I usually lead someone into the baptism of the Holy

Spirit.

Witness: Now that you have made Jesus Lord, you want to receive all He died to give. You want the power He has provided for you to be a witness and live a victorious Christian life. When Jesus was preparing to depart from this planet, He gave His disciples a final and most important commandment. *"And, being assembled together with them, commanded them that they should not depart from Jerusalem, but wait for the promise of the Father, which, saith he, ye have heard of me. For John truly baptized with water; but ye shall be baptized with the Holy Ghost not many days hence. And, when he had spoken these things, while they beheld, he was taken up, and a cloud received him out of their sight. But ye shall receive power, after that the Holy Ghost is come upon you; and ye shall be witnesses unto me..."* (Acts 1:4,5,9,8).

Witness: Are you willing to receive what Jesus died to give you?

Believer: Yes? (Usually a little reluctant)

Witness: (Read Acts 2: 1-4). *"And when the day of Pentecost was fully come, they were all with one accord in one place. And suddenly there came a sound from heaven as of a rushing mighty wind, and it filled all the house where they were sitting. And there appeared unto them cloven tongues*

*like as of fire, and it sat upon each of them.
And they were all filled with the Holy
Ghost, and began to speak with other
tongues, as the Spirit gave them utterance.*" The Bible says they were in one
accord. We are in one accord because we
are here for the same purpose. Do you
believe this promise is valid for you today?

Believer: I am not really sure.

Witness: Jesus Himself said for the disciples to receive this so they would have power. Because Jesus is your Lord, you should follow Him in all He instructed. (New believers are usually very pleased to follow the
Lord. There may, however, be a need to
share some additional scriptures.)

Witness: Verse 3 says the Holy Spirit came upon
them. It does not say that He came in them.
The Holy Spirit came in you when you got
saved. There is nothing to fear. He is in
you and wants to flow out to the world
through you.

Witness: The Bible says in verse 4, they were all
filled with the Holy Spirit. The word
"filled" does not mean they got more of,
but means they yielded to the influence of
the Holy Spirit. The Holy Spirit who came
in them when they got saved was now
going to begin to influence them and give
them the ability to speak in another lan-

guage. It is a language they do not know, but verse 11 says that some people recognized what they were saying and they were worshipping and praising God.

Witness: Are you afraid of tongues?

Believer: A little.

Witness: Do not be afraid, they are already in you. Tongues came in you when you got saved. They came in with the Holy Spirit. Now they are going to come out of you in prayer, praise and worship to our God. You will not understand it, but the Bible teaches that when we do this we become edified, or built up. When you begin to feel weak, you can do this and you will become stronger. The Bible says this is for all believers, "*And these signs shall follow them that believe...they shall speak with new tongues...*" Mark 16:17.

Witness: Do you believe this is for every believer?

Believer: Yes?

Witness: Do you believe this is for you?

Believer: (If yes, proceed. If no, answer questions. If not sure, proceed with caution). (If the believer is not positive at this point, faith must be built by teaching, attending worship services where people worship in tongues, and encouragement. Do not get pushy.)

Witness: Do you believe Jesus will keep His word to baptize you in the Holy Spirit just like He kept his promise to save you?

Believer: Yes.

Witness: Does Jesus ever lie?

Believer: No.

Witness: Then you believe He will hear your prayer tonight to be baptized in the Holy Spirit?

Believer: Yes.

Witness: Then we will pray and Jesus will do His part. He will baptize you in the Holy Spirit, right?

Believer: Right

Witness: Since He is going to do His part and baptize you in the Holy Spirit, are you going to do your part and speak in tongues?

Believer: I hope so.

Witness: Remember, we said they were yielded to the influence of the Holy Spirit. He did not make them do anything. But, as they prayed and worshipped God, they began to be drawn into praying in other tongues. But they had to open their mouth and speak. He did not make them speak; He led them to speak. They spoke as they yielded to the Spirit of God. After we pray, the Holy Spirit inside you will begin to compel you to worship God. When this happens, do not try to do it in you own language; that will be very frustrating. Simply speak. Verse four said they spoke...the Holy Spirit gave the utterance. It is the Spirit's job to form the words as you speak.

Believer: Yes I am. (Keep in mind, I have asked them two important questions. Are you going to receive? Are you going to speak? If they are not positive about both of these, do not pray for them; they are not operating faith. You will damage your faith and theirs if you proceed prematurely. But if they say yes, proceed as follows.)

Witness: I am going to lead you in a prayer. You pray unto the Lord, and He will hear you. After we have prayed, I will lay hands on you, then you stop praying in English and yield to the Holy Spirit. It is your job to speak and His job to form the words. Are you ready?

Believer: Yes? (If there are any questions at this point, take time to answer them.)

Witness: (I always reaffirm their salvation through this prayer.) Father...I thank you that Jesus died for my sins...I thank You that You raised Him from the dead...Jesus, you are my Lord...My life belongs to you...You promised to baptize me in the Holy Spirit...You promised I could receive power and speak in other tongues...When hands are laid on me...I will receive the baptism in the Holy Spirit...And I will worship you in other tongues...Thank you Holy Spirit that as I speak, you will form the words...

At this point, I get them to worship the Lord. When I feel a release, I lay hands on them and command them to be baptized in the Holy Spirit and speak in other tongues. I usually begin praying in tongues at that time, and they receive. If they are timid or reluctant, I do not rush them. Be patient and sensitive to the Holy Spirit.

It is important for them to speak in tongues at this time. If not, they will lose their confidence. If for some reason they do not speak in tongues, I encourage them and tell them they can any time they are ready. I have received many wonderful reports from those who went home and began to worship and pray in tongues at home. Some people are more comfortable in private than public. Never tell a person they have not received because they do not pray in tongues. Be an encourager.

Remember that it is only your job to proclaim, and it is the Holy Spirit's job to produce. Once you have told them the truth, it is up to them to believe and receive. Walk in love and be patient...they always come around.

While ministering in a recent meeting, a young

man visited from another church. He had a need for deliverance. The nature of the sin dictated that we should minister to him in private. After he was set free from demonic bondage, I explained the need for him to receive the baptism in the Holy Spirit.

This was against everything his denomination taught. However, he had just received deliverance from demonic bondage, which was something he could not get through his particular church. He knew he needed more power in his life. Yet there was reluctance on his part.

After the prayer, he was like many people; he resisted the Holy Spirit. People always feel compelled to pray in tongues after they have prayed the prayer of faith, but many, because of fear, will quench the Holy Spirit.

In this case I felt if I pushed it, he would run in fear. I looked him in the eye with love, confidence and firmness, and said, "I know you resisted the Holy Spirit. You had to refrain from speaking in other tongues. This is between you and God, however, and you will have to settle this with Him. This desire is going to continue to work in you unless you keep resisting. If you continue to resist, you will harden your heart against the Holy Spirit, and the desire will leave you. When you are alone praying and this desire is present, yield to the Holy Spirit." The next night he came to church beaming. "Last night," he said, "my little boy was sick. When I prayed for him, I began to pray in other tongues." Not only did he receive his prayer language, but also his son was healed.

I have seen people receive the baptism in the Holy Spirit dozens of different ways. I never try to put

God in a box. When ministering in any area, I want to stay sensitive to what the Holy Spirit says. I have had crusades where we prayed for people one at a time. Then I have had crusades where we prayed for people in masses.

While ministering in Honduras, people were responding every night by the hundreds. Each night after praying the sinners' prayer with those who responded, we would pray for those who wanted to receive the baptism in the Holy Spirit. The number of people responding was so large we could not pray for them individually.

As we prayed together in mass, it was like the day of Pentecost. More than a thousand people at one time were baptized in the Holy Spirit and spoke in other tongues.

Once, while trying to pioneer a new work, I had a man come to the clothing store where I worked. (Often while pioneering a new work, I would get a job to meet my financial needs, as well as, meet new people in the community.) He introduced himself and said, "I heard that you were able to cast demons out of people." I calmly answered, "Yes." He continued, "My father is a minister. I am a Christian, but I have never been completely free from homosexuality. Can you help me?" Immediate direction came from the Lord; "In three days I will be conducting a home prayer meeting. You fast for those three days and come to that meeting. I will break the power of the devil that is working in your life."

When the night of the meeting came, he was there. I did not announce to anyone what his need was. When it came time to minister to people I simply called him forward. I laid hands on him and said, "Satan, I break your power over _____, release him now in Jesus name." Without me saying another word, he began to rejoice and worship God. He knew that he was free. Without anyone ministering to him or teaching him, he began to worship in other tongues. This was something he had never seen.

Always have a Biblical objective in ministry. But let the Holy Spirit establish the particular method of ministry. If He does not lead in a particular direction, just follow your basic plan.

22

Casting Out Devils

A part of the reason the Spirit came upon you was to "*...preach deliverance to the captives...*" Luke 4:18. The word for captive means "prisoner of war." We are to proclaim the good news to the prisoners of war, "Your freedom has been purchased; you do not have to remain a captive."

Isaiah prophesies it this way, "*To open the blind eyes, to bring out the prisoners from the prison, and them that sit in darkness out of the prison house.*" Isaiah 42:7. Not only do we proclaim their freedom; we are to bring them out of the prison house that is holding them. We are to break the darkness that blinds them by exposing them to the light of God's truth.

Healing and deliverance were two of the most powerful and effective tools Jesus gave us for evangelism. It is these gifts that remove one from the realm of argument to the realm of power. Anyone can present a good argument, but only truth will set people free from the yoke of oppression. Regardless of the opposition, one can never present a persuasive argument against real results.

Keep in mind that you have not entered the realm of ministry until you are setting people free.

Until then, you are just talking. *"For the kingdom of God is not in word* (talk)*, but in power."* 1 Corinthians 4:20. The world has heard enough about God. They do not want to hear about God. They need to experience God. In a world that has heard nothing but judgement and condemnation, they will have to experience God's goodness to believe it. What greater love could one experience than to know their sin and their demons cannot cut them off from the love of God? Even when they are slaves to their sins, Jesus will not only love them, but He will set them free and give them a new life.

A major portion of Jesus' ministry was casting out devils. Jesus knew that where there was oppression, there were devils. Acts 10:38 says, *"How God anointed Jesus of Nazareth with the Holy Ghost and with power; who went about doing good, and healing all that were oppressed of the devil; for God was with him."* Demons only have the ability to oppress those who do not believe the truth. The religious community of Jesus' day, like today, kept people in bondage through fear. But Jesus always taught the truth, which broke the control, and then cast out the demon.

In Mark 16:17 it says, *"And these signs shall follow them that believe: In my name shall they cast out devils..."* This was a part of the commission that Jesus gave us when He sent us forth to win the world. We have wanted to reach the world by becoming socially accepted and influential. What we have wound up with is a bunch of socially-accepted, demon-oppressed people influencing the church. What good does it do to reach people and get them in our churches if we do not set them free?

The powerless church has paved the way for New Age and other cult growth. We have been told the supernatural would turn people off. Yet, people are flocking by the thousands to every new cult that promises the supernatural. Man was created in the image of an all-powerful, supernatural God. We have a need for the supernatural. If the church does not meet that need, an imposter will.

Casting out devils does not have to be a far out, "spooky" ministry. Moreover, it should never become the main focus of ministry. It is a tool, a means to an end; it is not the end. If deliverance becomes the main focus of our ministry, it will become something that is unhealthy and destructive.

Jesus showed that insanity, physical sickness and sin itself could be the result of demonic oppression. This does not mean, however, that every person in these situations needs deliverance. We will attempt to demonstrate how to minister in this area without extremes.

One of the questions most people ask is this, "When do I know if someone needs deliverance?" For our purposes, the word "deliverance" will be used of breaking any type of demonic stronghold or activity. It is nonessential to differentiate between possession, oppression, bondage or any other terminology. Regardless of the terminology, they need to be set free.

Many people are instantly set free from demonic bondage when they are saved; however, some are not. The difference is in what one is able to believe for at the time of salvation. 1 Peter 1:9 clearly shows that you receive the end or goal of your faith. *"Receiving the end of your faith, even the salvation of your souls.*" Those that are not made completely free must trust God in new areas of life to find freedom.

Prior to being born again, I was under extreme demonic bondage. In fact, I was a slave to certain types of spirits that were ruling my life. When I gave my life to Jesus, it was absolute. I held nothing back. I was sick of me and sick of all my life had become. Because of the absolute commitment to Lordship, I was set free from that demonic control.

It has been my observation that a person will sometimes "hold on to" an area of their life. There is not total surrender in every area. The result is a stronghold that must ultimately be broken. In many cases, this will require deliverance.

I have four basic ways that I determine when there is a need for deliverance: (1) When the demon manifests itself, (2) when there is uncontrollable behavior, (3) by a gift of the Holy Spirit, (4) when the person requests deliverance. There are no "sure fire" indicators other than these. An attempt to assign certain types of sin to a demon is not consistent with scripture. In Galatians 5:19-21, we have a list of the works of the flesh. The sins are the result of the flesh, but almost any Charismatic or Pentecostal would be quick to try to cast out a devil for any of the symptoms. *"Now the works of the flesh are manifest, which are these; adultery, fornication, uncleanness, lasciviousness, Idolatry, witchcraft, hatred, variance, emulations, wrath, strife, seditions, heresies, envyings, murders, drunkenness, revelings, and such like; of the which I tell you before, as I have also told you in time past, that they which do such things shall not inherit the kingdom of God."* If a person is involved in any of these sins, we know there is a flesh problem. We do not know if there is a demon problem.

Keep in mind that whether it is or is not a demon the person will ultimately have to conquer the flesh. Until grace is appropriated to conquer the sin, there is no lasting victory. Therefore, all deliverance should be followed up by instructions on walking in the grace of God.[1]

The presence and power of the Lord is the greatest way I know of to threaten and expose demons. Mark gives a perfect example of a demon manifesting itself in the presence of the Lord. *"But when he saw Jesus afar off, he ran and worshipped him, And cried with a loud voice, and said, What have I to do with thee, Jesus, thou Son of the Most High God? I adjure thee by God, that thou torment me not."* Mark 5:6-7. This is one of many times that demons became so disturbed that they manifested themselves in the presence of Jesus.

The Book of Psalms is full of tremendous promises of the enemy fleeing and being destroyed because of the presence of the Lord. I can only assume that the presence of the Lord so threatens the security of the demon, its fear causes it to react.

Several years ago while having a worship service in my home, a demon began to manifest itself. A nine-year-old girl jumped to her feet and began to cry out, "Get out of me, you cannot stay in me, I do not want you in me." We immediately took authority over the spirit and continued to worship. No one did any-

---

[1] *"Grace: The Power to Change"* Dr. James B. Richards, Impact International Publications, Huntsville, Alabama

thing to prompt the child's actions, but the presence of God was unbearable for this spirit.

My experience has proven that an atmosphere of praise and worship is the easiest place to accomplish any type of healing or deliverance. The presence of God adequately demobilizes all spirits. Psalms 68:2 says, *"As smoke is driven away, so drive them away; as wax melteth before the fire, so let the wicked perish at the presence of God."*

When a demon manifests itself is the easiest time to bring about deliverance. It seems that an outward manifestation is a last, great attempt to produce fear and maintain control. I have always viewed outward manifestation as a final sign of weakness and fear on the part of the spirit.

When these demons manifest, there is no need to talk with them; you need not know their name. You do not need to know how many there are. Simply command it to come out in Jesus' name. The Scripture does not support much of what we are taught to do in deliverance. Jesus did not ask every demon its name; neither did He assign every demon a place to go.

If the devil cannot produce fear in you by his manifestation, there is yet another trap to avoid: SENSATIONALISM. Do not give into what I call "charismatic theatrics." Many people are drawn into various types of sensationalism that reduce the chances of real freedom and actually give rise to fear and more demonic control.

When a devil manifests itself, it may growl, become violent, scream, and commit immoral actions or a host of things. But keep in mind, "it is just an ignorant, wimpy devil," regardless of what it does.

You have all authority over all demons, regardless of how big their bark may be.

In more than 25 years of ministry, I have never had a devil overpower me. Only once have I ever had a physical confrontation. Even that could have been avoided if I had known. You receive what you believe for. Since I do not believe a demon can overpower me, cast me to the ground or harm me, IT CANNOT! Much of that is simply theatrics that we give in to because of ignorance.

Uncontrollable behavior is a fairly consistent indicator of demonic activity. As one preacher said, "When you are out of control, the devil is in control." God commands you to be in control, and He certainly does not forcibly take control of you. But the devil always desires to dominate and control through deceit, lust, fear and unbelief.

When I deal with anyone who is uncontrollable, irrational or unreasonable, I usually find a demon. Until they are free from demonic control, they will not regain control of their actions and emotions. The Bible speaks of being vexed. One of the meanings of the word "vex" is "consumed." When anyone is consumed, they are out of control.

When someone comes to me requesting deliverance, I am quick to assist. People know when they need help. *"And, behold, a woman of Canaan came out of the same coasts, and cried unto him, saying, Have mercy on me, O Lord, thou son of David; my daughter is grievously vexed with a devil."* Matthew 15:22. More than once, people came to Jesus requesting deliverance. We should never take such a request lightly. This, of course, does not mean that every person desiring deliverance actually needs it.

A gift of the Holy Spirit is the most accurate way of recognizing the need for deliverance. Many times there will be a word of knowledge that will reveal the need. Always submit words of knowledge. Do not insist to be absolutely correct with every word of knowledge. It is easy for us to "miss it" occasionally. The most accurate gift for deliverance is discerning of spirits.

When the discerning of spirits works in my life, I usually see the spirit and see how it has attached itself to the person. In these cases, I see when it leaves. Like all of the gifts, I cannot make it work when I desire, but I am always open for it. Discerning of spirits did not work in me for years, yet during that time I still had success in the area of deliverance. I simply operated in the areas I had confidence. Do not think you need a special gift for this ministry. Jesus said this was for all believers.

The first time discerning of spirits worked in my life was while praying for a baby. I had led the parents to the Lord several months before. When their baby was born, it had some difficulties. After praying for quite a long time, I had a vision. In the vision I saw two little spirits attached to the baby's lungs. I went to the parents and shared the word with them. They brought the baby from the hospital nursery, prayed for him, and he was healed.

The Book of Acts shows the operation of the Holy Spirit in the apostle Paul to bring about deliverance. *"And it came to pass, as we went to prayer, a certain damsel possessed with a spirit of divination met us, which brought her masters much gain by soothsaying. The same followed Paul and us, and cried, saying, These men are the servants of the Most High God, who show unto us the way of salvation. And this did she many days. But Paul, being grieved, turned and said to the spirit, I command thee, in the name of Jesus Christ, to come out of her. And he came out the same hour."* Acts 16:16-18.

The girl with this spirit followed him, shouting out, for many days. Yet he did nothing! Why? He did not know she had a demon. It was not until he became grieved inwardly that he realized the need for deliverance. Paul did not claim to be omniscient; he simply followed the Holy Spirit. Likewise, we will not always know who has a demon. This is not proof of spirituality.

When ministering deliverance, I first pinpoint the need. If I get a word of knowledge or discernment, I share it with the person in a kind, merciful manner. I want the person to acknowledge the need. Even when the young boy in Mark 9:20 fell on the ground and went into a convulsion, Jesus remained calm and dealt with the problem. Likewise, do not let the person's actions dictate how you will minister; follow the Holy Spirit.

Many times while ministering deliverance, the person will "fake" passing out. I make them open their eyes and talk to me. I make them ask for help. I make them confess their sin, and I make them take authority over the devil and the sin. Their will must be involved.

It is important to realize that bondage is always linked to beliefs. Many people feel they have committed some sin that is so great that God cannot forgive them. It is not the power of the devil that keeps them bound. It is the power of this belief. Their need to confess is primarily so they will break that belief. When they confess and experience love and mercy, the destructive power of that belief is broken.

From that position of openness and honesty, they are able to have a new confidence in themselves and God. They must get their will involved. They must use their own authority.

When their will is not involved you spend hours attempting to bring about a deliverance that will soon be lost. If they do not want it, do not try to force it. Many ministers waste great amounts of valuable time with those who want attention--not help. Once word gets out (through "hell's hot-line") every code-pendent, attention-desperate flake will show up at your door to rob your time, energy and joy.

After they have gotten their will involved, I boldly command the spirit to leave them in Jesus' name. More importantly, I get them to take authority. I will take authority and worship until I sense a release in my heart. Many times I will see into the spirit realm and know when the spirit leaves. Otherwise, I continue until I have a release in my heart. I never use any outward sign or manifestation to determine if there is freedom. The devil will use outward manifestations to trick you. If they fall down, I either make them stand back up or I kneel over them and continue, but I refuse to quit until there is freedom

One day a young man involved in homosexual-ity came to me for help. After sharing with him, I told him what I was going to do. I led him in confession and prayer, and then I began to take authority over the spirit. He sat and looked at me like I was crazy. I worshipped for a few minutes and commanded the spirit to come out. He never changed; he sat there looking at me like I had two heads. This continued for about twenty minutes. Finally, he dove across a table and began to shake violently.

I continued to command that spirit to come out until I had a witness in my heart he was free. While one must be committed to seeing this process through to victory, we should also realize that this should not take forever.

When a deliverance session takes too long, it usually indicates a lack of willingness or cooperation. In these cases, one must not continually scream at the devil; instead, he should address the beliefs of the person.

After setting someone free, I have him or her to begin thanking God for freedom. I show them how to worship. I usually lead them into the baptism in the Holy Spirit right then. I teach them how to resist the devil by exercising faith in God's Word. I warn them of the consequences of becoming involved with past sins. Then I always insist they get into a good "Spirit-filled" church.

If a person receives deliverance and does not follow through with a godly lifestyle and sound teaching, they will usually fall prey to the same bondage again. Ultimately, they have to conquer that problem with the flesh. They must learn to win over sin.

Be sure to resist the temptation to theatrics. I prefer to take people away from the crowd for this type of ministry. I do not want to instill fear in the crowd, nor do I desire to embarrass the person.

23

Healing the Sick

Healing the sick was one of the most powerful and persuasive aspects of Jesus' ministry. The sick being healed is a clear demonstration of God's love. Setting man free from the pain of physical suffering gave an absolute witness to His claims of God's great love for mankind.

Until the time of Jesus, sickness was viewed as God's punishment on mankind. The self-righteous, religious leaders, therefore, had no compassion for the suffering of the people. Jesus, on the other hand, identified sickness as a work of the devil. *"How God anointed Jesus of Nazareth with the Holy Ghost and with power; who went about doing good, and HEALING ALL THAT WERE OPPRESSED OF THE DEVIL; for God was with him."* Acts 10:38.

Jesus began His ministry with healing and continued to do so until the end of His earthly ministry, and there was never a person He refused to heal. *"And Jesus went about all Galilee, teaching in their synagogues, and preaching the gospel of the kingdom, and healing all manner of sickness and all manner of disease among the people. And his fame went through-*

out all Syria; and they brought unto him all sick people that were taken with divers diseases and torments, and those which were possessed with devils, and those which were lunatic, and those that had the palsy; and he healed them." Matthew 4:23-24.

Jesus taught His disciples to heal the sick and sent them forth on two different occasions with a commission to preach, heal and deliver. In Matthew 10:7-8 He sent out the twelve and said, *"And as ye go, preach, saying, The kingdom of heaven is at hand. Heal the sick, cleanse the lepers, raise the dead, cast out devils; freely ye have received, freely give."*

Mark puts it like this, *"And he ordained twelve, that they should be with him, and that he might send them forth to preach, And to have power to heal sicknesses, and to cast out devils."* Mark 3:14-15.

The twelve were not the only ones given the commission to preach and heal. *"After these things the Lord appointed other seventy also, and sent them two and two before his face into every city and place, whither he himself would come. And heal the sick that are therein, and say unto them, The kingdom of God is come nigh unto you."* Luke 10:1,9. Jesus intended for all men who preached the gospel to perform the gospel.

Before departing planet earth, Jesus made it clear that the ministry of healing should continue. *"And he said unto them, Go ye into all the world, and preach the gospel to every creature. And these signs shall follow them that believe; In my name shall they...lay hands on the sick, and they shall recover."* Mark 16:15,17,18. This was not a commission for the people of a certain era or dispensation; this was a commission for THOSE WHO BELIEVE!

The early church took this commission seriously and went forth preaching and healing the sick. *"And they went forth, and preached everywhere, the Lord working with them, and confirming the word with signs following. Amen."* Mark 16:20. The great revival in Jerusalem in Acts 3 was the result of a healing. Samaria was reached in Acts 8 because of healings and miracles. In the early church, there was no separating the gospel from healing. The good news for the sick was the fact that God did not make them sick; moreover, He made them well.

Healing is a vital part of all personal ministry. As I have conducted crusades in foreign countries, it has been the healing of the sick that opened the door for the gospel. When preaching to people who have never heard the gospel, you only have an argument if there is no demonstration of power. When the sick are healed, the goodness of God demonstrated draws the people to repentance. *"Or despisest thou the riches of his [goodness] and forbearance and longsuffering; not knowing that the [goodness] of God leadeth thee to [repentance]?"* Romans 2:4. The religious myth that sickness is from God still holds people captive in America and around the world. The demonstration of God's healing power is a testimony to His love for man.

While ministering in a mountainous village in Mexico, healing was the key to reaching the entire village. This particular village had been very difficult to reach. Previous teams had not been able to penetrate the many opposing factors. So, we divided into teams and went house to house. At each house, we introduced ourselves and talked to the people about the

evening meeting. Then we would ask if there was any
sickness in the family. When they brought the sick, we
would pray for them. Because of the multitudes that
were healed, the whole village let out for the meeting.
They received the gospel and multitudes were saved.

In America the healing ministry is somewhat
affected by the attitudes of the people. The preachers
have conditioned society and the church against miracles.   Our educational system has conditioned the
world against the supernatural power of God. People's
attitudes greatly affect the power of God in their own
lives. Jesus faced this same problem. *"And he could
there do no mighty work, save that he laid his hands
upon a few sick folks, and healed them. And he mar-
veled because of their unbelief. And he went round
about the villages, teaching."* Mark 6:5-6. Some
scholars interpret this as, "he laid hands upon a few
sick folk with minor problems and healed them." The
point is this: the magnitude of the miracles was determined by their unbelief. It did not say He **would** do
NO mighty works, it said He **COULD** DO NO
MIGHTY WORKS. He was limited by their beliefs.

As you move into this area of ministry, keep
this in mind: healing is not something that happens
because you have reached a certain level of holiness or
anointing. In nine out of fourteen one-on-one cases,
Jesus clearly pointed out that people were healed because of THEIR FAITH...not His. We merely proclaim the Word. They must believe it.

Secondly, God is not confirming you or your
ministry because people get healed. He is confirming
the Word. *"And they went forth, and preached every
where, the Lord working with them, and confirming the*

word with signs following. Amen." Mark 16:20. The word "them" is not in the original text. What God worked with and confirmed was the Word. When we preach the promises of healing, God can and will confirm it to those who believe the Word.

The idea of a man having a "special anointing" or God confirming his ministry has destroyed and belittled the healing ministry in our day. Healing has nothing to do with your anointing, holiness or personal character. Healing is a product of preaching the truth about God's desire to heal and people believing that truth.

Thirdly, healing is not a specialized ministry. The healing ministry demonstrates and confirms the love of God. It is for all people, but it should never become an end within itself. Healing is a powerful tool for reaching the world. It should never be confined to the four walls of the church. Nor should we limit the scope of our ministry to healing. We should follow Jesus' example of teaching and ministry.

When ministering healing one-on-one, we should always try to build faith in the hearer. *"So, then, faith cometh by hearing, and hearing by the word of God."* Romans 10:17. We must teach specific scriptures that promise healing. I have found it to be of the utmost importance to show healing as a part of the work of the cross. If it is viewed in any other capacity, it will be approached in works instead of faith. When people see it as a finished work of the cross, it becomes quite easy to receive. At the same time that Jesus conquered sin he conquered sickness.

Galatians 3:13 teaches that Jesus delivered us from ALL the curse of the law. The moment He set us free from the power of sin, He set us free from the power of sickness.

Never get in a rush about healing. Unless the Lord clearly leads or the person requests it, I take my time. We cannot pray the prayer of faith until they believe. Once a person believes healing is theirs, it is essential that they know how to walk it out. When a person is convinced of the promise, the problem is never the lack of faith; it is usually the lack of knowing how to operate faith.

In Acts 14 we see a clear example of someone having the faith but not knowing how to operate their faith. *"And there sat a certain man at Lystra, impotent in his feet, being a cripple from his mother's womb, who never had walked. The same heard Paul speak; who, stedfastly beholding him, and perceiving that he had faith to be healed, Said with a loud voice, Stand upright on thy feet. And he leaped and walked."* Acts 14:8-10. This man had the faith, but he was still crippled. Paul forced him to operate his faith by doing the very thing he believed he could not do.

Faith is more than believing. It is a believing that commits to and implements truth. James said it this way, *"Even so faith, if it hath not works, is dead, being alone. Yea, a man may say, Thou hast faith, and I have works; show me thy faith without thy works, and I will show thee my faith by my works. Thou believest that there is one God; thou doest well. The devils also believe, and tremble. But wilt thou know, O vain man, that faith without works is dead? Was not Abraham, our father, justified by works, when he had offered Isaac, his son, upon the altar? Seest thou how faith wrought with his works, and by works was faith made perfect?"* James 2:17-22.

Once a person prays the prayer of faith for healing, he should begin to do what he could not do. Paul perceived the man had faith to be healed, but he would have remained crippled if he had not moved from the realm of dead faith to perfect faith. Dead faith waits for a sign or feeling. Perfect faith acts and becomes a sign. A works mentality will do something trying to get God to heal them. Perfect faith believes the promise and knows that healing is already his. Perfect faith is not trying to prove anything, it is not waiting on anything; it simply believes in the finished work of the cross and responds.

I often help the cripples stand. I take them by the shoulders and help them start walking. Before long, they are walking under their own power. When people respond to my altar calls for healing, I have them start doing what they could not have done before the prayer of faith. For many it is difficult or even painful at first, but as they trust God for their healing and continue, the power of God is released. They become able to do what the Word says they can do.

In a recent meeting, I was praying for people who had difficulty moving their joints. Several of them had pain in their knees. I held their hands while they bent their knees all the way to the floor, then I held them while they stood back upright. For many, it was so painful that they began to weep. I told them to keep trusting God for their healing. Many of them walked away healed.

I encourage them to thank God for their healing. Faith is a matter of the heart. When people begin to do what their bodies say they cannot do, the pain and the difficulty will overpower their hearts. If their heart becomes overwhelmed, they will never walk in their healing. By continuing to thank God for their healing, they are in fact guarding and strengthening faith in their hearts. If they will keep their hearts in faith, healing will flow.

People must know they are not trying to get God to act. They must believe that the life and power of God is already in them. It came in when Jesus came. For the believer, healing is a past tense reality. They need to trust God and experience healing.

The real key to healing is the realization that Jesus purchased it through His death, burial and resurrection. He poured it into us when the Spirit of God came to live in us. It is already ours. We are not trying to get God to respond to us. We are simply responding to what God has already done.

It is essential to teach a person to resist sickness if it comes back. Sickness, just like sin, will always try to come back. If one does not know how to resist sickness, it will regain a stronghold. Therefore, we should teach people to resist it. Too often, we have created a lifestyle that uses sickness as a way to avoid responsibilities. The person struggling with guilt believes sickness is their punishment. There are many beliefs that facilitate sickness. In the chapter on follow-up, I will discuss the different follow-up cards we use. Proper follow-up is essential if our fruit is to remain. *"Ye have not chosen me, but I have chosen you, and ordained you, that ye should go and bring forth fruit, and that your fruit should remain: that whatsoever ye shall ask of the Father in my name, he may give it you."* John 15:16.

When I was trying to conquer a lifelong kidney disorder, I would experience healing. But I did not know what to do when the problem reoccurred. When the symptoms returned, I thought, "Well, I must not really be healed." That type of believing would facilitate sickness. On several occasions, I would leave the hospital or get up out of a sick bed supernaturally, only to be overcome at a later time. When I learned how to resist sickness, it could not come back on me, and I remained healed.

Therefore, we teach the Word, pray the prayer of faith, and have them put works with their faith. When praying the prayer of faith, I lead the individual in scriptural confessions of God's promise for healing. Then I lead them in commanding the sickness to leave their body. While they are putting works with their faith, I lead them in praise and thanksgiving. By having them do all these things, they know it is their faith that got them healed.

If they think it is my faith, they will never maintain their healing in the future. They will think they need someone to bring the promises of God to them. This way, they realize God hears their prayers. They do not become dependent on me; no one other than God can get the glory.

One of our Bible school students was driving home one night after a meeting. Along the road he saw a man walking on crutches. He stopped, witnessed to him about the Lord and told him about healing. He prayed for the man, got him to start walking without his crutches and in a few minutes he was walking freely.

These kinds of healing are frequent with our

students and church members. They have taken the mysticism out of healing. It has become as simple as getting a person born again. If you will stick to these simple procedures, you will begin to see results. The best place to start is on you. If you have physical needs, follow this same plan.

First, fill your heart with scriptural promises for healing. When you are sure it is yours through Christ, lay hands on yourself and command sickness to leave. Worship God in confession of the scriptures and thank Him for your healing. See yourself healed. See yourself doing things you have not been able to do. Then begin to do what you see in your heart. If it hurts or is difficult, keep speaking the Word. If you do not see immediate results, speak the Word several times a day in worship and praise. Spend time meditating on the promises of God. Persuade your heart of the reality of health and healing.[1]

It was healing in my own life that gave me the courage to go out and get others healed. Begin ministering healing to others. It will be just as powerful whether you start with yourself or someone else. You are a believer, and these signs will follow you if you preach the Word about healing. You will "lay hands on the sick and they SHALL recover."

---

[1] *"Taking the Limits Off God"*, James B. Richards,
    Impact International Publications, Huntsville,
    Alabama

24

Follow-Up

"*And Jesus came and spake unto them, saying, All power is given unto me in heaven and in earth. Go ye, therefore, and teach all nations, baptizing them in the name of the Father, and of the Son, and of the Holy Ghost: Teaching them to observe all things whatsoever I have commanded you: and, lo, I am with you always, even unto the end of the world. Amen.*" Matthew 28: 18-20. The Great Commission starts with making converts.

The second part is to teach or disciple those we reach. It should be our goal to disciple everyone. Our commitment to make disciples should be just as fervent as our commitment to win the lost. Unfortunately, it seems that most churches are good at one or the other. But there is no reason we cannot be effective at both.

Combining the two aspects of the Great Commission is not difficult if we have them both properly defined. There is little difficulty in defining evangelism, but the views on discipleship vary dramatically.

The best way to understand discipleship is to look at the ministry of Jesus. Jesus had a two-fold approach to training His disciples. First, He taught the Word, then He allowed them to participate in hands-on training. They would watch Him perform miracles. They saw Him cast out devils. He never taught them anything that He did not model. Then, He would send them forth to do what He had modeled.[1]

This is completely opposite of the way we train people today. Because most ministers never do anything except preach and counsel, their members seldom see the Word of God modeled. Because they do not see it operated, there is mysticism about application. Therefore, they usually never apply the Word. They always feel there is some secret technique.

Jesus never left his disciples in the realm of theory. He always showed them how to make it work. For some reason, the vast majority of people cannot translate information into application. Therefore, the effective leader will always provide practical training. Jesus always allowed His disciples to watch Him minister. On occasion, He limited participation to the more mature, but He always trained as He went.

Philippians 3:16 in the NIV says, "*Only let us live up to what we have already attained.*" Maturity, for the Christian, is not the amount of knowledge one has obtained. Maturity is the amount of knowledge one can **apply**. Truth does not set people free. Putting truth into practice sets people free. "*Then said Jesus to those Jews, which believed on him, If ye continue in my word, then are ye my disciples indeed: And ye shall know the truth, and the truth shall make you free.*" John 8:31-32. To continue means to "hold to" and "put

----

[1] For a more complete rendering of Jesus' method of making disciples, see "*Leadership That Builds People, Volume II: Developing Leaders Around You,*" James B. Richards, Impact International Publications, Huntsville, Alabama

into practice."

In Philippians 4:9, Paul said to DO what we have learned in order to experience God's peace. *"Those things, which ye have both learned, and received, and heard, and seen in me, do: and the God of peace shall be with you."* To do is to know. You do not really know anything you have not done. We, on the other hand, think we should not do anything until we know all there is to know about it. Thus, we are confined to a life of theory.

Consequently, the best way to disciple someone is to give them truth along with opportunity to function in that truth. It is of special value for them to see you operate the truth you have taught them. We must stick to Jesus' plan: teach the Word, model the Word we teach; watch them operate the Word; then send them out with someone else as a team. This is the process in making disciples.

Because the new convert becomes actively involved in the ministry he is receiving, he is gaining practical application. He is finding out how to exercise faith. It is not a theory for him. He will not call you the first time something goes wrong. He is immediately becoming aware of the fact that he needs Jesus more than he needs you. This is one of those revelations our ego does not want to accept.

We must shun the temptation to make men disciples unto ourselves. This happens when we do everything for the new believer. "Let me do that for you" are words of death. When we portray ourselves as the "faith men", and we do all the praying and all the "spiritual stuff," we impress them so much that they think they need us to get to God. This mentality has been in the church since the Dark Ages. The dependency on clergy is nothing more than a manipulative, codependent tactic for control.[1] We think if we keep people dependent on us, they will stay in our churches. By so doing, we destroy that person's future. We cripple them before they have ever learned to stand. They never become productive for the Kingdom of God or develop a confidence of Christ in them.

When we involve the believer in the ministry, they quickly realize that we are helpers, but the real activity is between God and themselves. They see it as their faith that has gotten them saved, healed or delivered. This type of ministry makes the believer more and more dependent on Jesus and less and less dependent on us. Moreover, a disciple is someone who can function independently of man because he is dependent on Jesus.[2]

Immediately after ministering to an individual, I try to give them a follow-up card that pertains to the area of ministry they have received. I simply read the side of the card that teaches them how to renew their mind. Then, I repeat the scriptures on the opposite side of the card. This is the first phase of follow-up.

The second phase of follow-up works similar to this: "I would like to bring you some more material to

---

[1] *"Escape from Codependent Christianity"* James B. Richards, Impact International Publications, Huntsville, Alabama

[2] *"My Church, My Family: How to Have a Healthy Relationship with the Church"* James B. Richards, Impact International Publications, Huntsville, Alabama

help you in your new walk with the Lord."[3] Then, I very casually and confidently ask for their address and phone number. They may not want to give you the phone number, but you can use a local directory or on-line computer services to cross-reference the address and phone number.

It is good to point out the church's phone number on the literature and encourage them to call if they have questions. In the case of ministry with a stranger, it would be wise to invite them to your local church. People are hesitant to come to a strange church with someone they do not know. However, the people you know will usually come with you.

At this point in time you can "plug them in" to whatever your local church follow-up system may be. I have found that having a cell group or Bible study in my own home is usually a powerful tool in bridging the gap between personal ministry and long-term discipleship.

We have a sponsoring program[4] for new converts and those who are new in God. To sponsor, one will request the opportunity to drop some materials by the person's house. When the sponsor arrives, he has a simple Bible study he conducts with the new believers. He requests the opportunity to come back next week. If all goes according to the plan, the sponsor will come for a total of six visits and conduct a simple Bible study each time. This creates a great foundation for the new

---

[3] Offer materials that will assist them in whatever area they have received ministry.

[4] "*Sponsor Workbook*," James B. Richards, Impact International Publications, Huntsville, Alabama

believer and often creates opportunity to reach the entire family.

At the earliest time possible, begin to reach into the new convert's circle of influence. This begins with the sponsor visits. Go with him to visit his friends and relatives. Help him witness to them. This is an excellent time to begin a new cell group in the new convert's home. Since his friends will be the ones influencing him to backslide, outreach to them will solve the problem. First, they may get saved. Second, if they do not get saved, they will probably avoid him in the future. Either case will be a blessing to the new convert.

When I was first saved, I got a deacon from the church to meet with all my "hippie" friends in my home. We had several of those meetings. Many of those friends got saved in those early home meetings. The ones who did not get saved avoided me like the plague, which kept me from many negative influences. Over the years, however, because of my clear-cut stand, many of those same people eventually contacted me for ministry. Many who initially rejected me are now committed believers.

I learned how to talk to people about the Lord by going with my deacon friend. I just watched at first. Before long, I wanted to talk a little. In a few weeks, I was going out alone. In a few months, I was reaching masses of people through one-on-one evangelism. Personal ministry was the training ground that led me into a worldwide ministry.

The discipline that changed my life more than anything else was being involved in personal ministry. I listened as my deacon friend answered questions. I saw how he handled people. When we had time alone I asked questions. He "took me under his wing." He invited me to his house regularly. We talked about the Bible, and we had fun.

It was the time I spent with him that helped to formulate my future in God. It was this discipline that affected my life far more than the church services. This is the way Jesus discipled, and it should be the way we disciple.

Anytime you teach a person anything, show them how to do it. When they are ready, have them do it while you observe. When you teach them about prayer, have a prayer meeting. When you teach them about witnessing, take them out witnessing. When you tell them about studying the Bible, have a Bible study together. Tell them, show them and involve them.

If people do not get to see you do it, they always think you are leaving something out. I have seen that the strongest, most effective Bible School students are the ones that get involved beyond the required amounts. They go with me on crusades, and they get active in church. They go out visiting with our follow-up leaders. They see and participate in what they are learning. They leave here totally independent of us and totally dependent on Jesus.

25

Restoring the Backslidden

A major portion of Jesus' ministry was to the backslidden. In Matthew 15:24 Jesus said, "*I am not sent but unto the lost sheep of the house of Israel.*" The word for "lost" means destroyed or marred. Many of the people were lost or destroyed in sin, but many were destroyed by the hardness of the religious system.

Isaiah 52:5 goes on to say, "*Now, therefore, what have I here, saith the LORD, that my people is taken away for nought? They that rule over them make them to howl, saith the LORD; and my name continually every day is blasphemed.*" Isaiah prophesied of the reproach brought on the name of the Lord because of the leaders. Verse 7 then gives a contrast to those hard negative leaders by saying, "*How beautiful upon the mountains are the feet of him that bringeth good tidings, that publisheth peace; that bringeth good tidings of good, that publisheth salvation; that saith unto Zion, Thy God reigneth!*" Isaiah 52:7. Legalism and judgement drive people away from the Lord. It always has, and it always will. Good news and peace, on the other hand, draw people to Him.

Much of the evangelism in America will al-

ways consist of reaching those who have been destroyed by the negative, judgmental religious system of
our day.   Many people backslide because of outright
sin.   But in the majority of those cases, sin came
because of the law, judgement and unbelief that they
were taught.

The only thing that will keep people from
turning to the world will be the promises of God,
which are provided by the Lord Jesus. 2 Peter 1:4 says,
*"Whereby are given unto us exceeding great and pre-
cious promises: that by these ye might be partakers of
the divine nature, having escaped the corruption that is
in the world through lust."*   One only escapes the lust
in the world by the precious promises of God, and the
gospel (good news) is that Jesus has qualified us to
receive those promises.

If the good news is not presented to people,
they will always turn back to the world for fulfillment.
If God is a faultfinding, judgmental, demanding God
who provides nothing for us, we will always go back to
the world.   But when we know the promises are ours,
we have no need to return to the world.   The corruption
in the world works by lust.   If we have all that pertains
to life and godliness, we would not lust (desire) anything the world has to offer.

Likewise, it will be the love of God and
promises of God that will restore the backslidden.   The
difficulty in restoring the individual, however, is the
fact that they still believe the message that destroyed
them.   The *"Gospel of Peace"* is the most effective
message I have heard for bringing restoration.[1]

---

[1] *"The Gospel of Peace,"*   James B. Richards, Impact
International Publications, Huntsville, Alabama

When the backslidden actually believe what Jesus did on the cross, freedom comes. The love of God is demonstrated in the message of the cross: Jesus became your sin, took your punishment, died in your place, and rose from the dead, giving you the free gift of righteousness and all the associated benefits. God is not mad at you, and He is not the source of your problems. This is the message the backslidden need to hear. They are convinced that God is angry. They are convinced that He is the source of their pain.

"To whom he said, This is the rest wherewith ye may cause the weary to rest; and this is the refreshing: yet they would not hear. But the word of the LORD was unto them precept upon precept, precept upon precept; line upon line, line upon line; here a little, and there a little; that they might go, and fall backward, and be broken, and snared, and taken." Isaiah 28:12-13. The backslidden need to enter into the rest that comes through the grace of the Lord. But they often choose to cling to law, line upon line, precept upon precept; therefore, they cannot enter into rest. The one thing the weary must have is rest. When he sees rest for his soul, he can be restored.

Only a consistent demonstration of the love of God will restore the backslider. Whether they are destroyed because of sin or loaded down with legalism, we must show them the love of God. For most, it is easier to love a backslider who did not affect you personally. I know of several churches that boast in reaching hurting people. They talk about it from the pulpit and make a great deal of it. But I have noticed they tend to only have mercy on the hurting people who did not hurt them.

When someone's sin affects us, we tend to proclaim judgement instead of restoration. We want to see them suffer because of what they have done to us. Galatians 6:1 appropriately reserves restoration ministry for the spiritual. *"Brethren, if a man be overtaken in a fault, ye which are spiritual, restore such an one in the spirit of meekness; considering thyself, lest thou also be tempted."* Restoration must be done in meekness and gentleness.

Beyond that, however, we must watch lest we be tempted. There is a temptation in the restoration ministry, and it was so common in the early church that the Holy Spirit had Paul to warn us. Galatians 6:2-4 continues, *"Bear ye one another's burdens, and so fulfill the law of Christ. For if a man think himself to be something, when he is nothing, he deceiveth himself. But let every man prove his own work, and then shall he have rejoicing in himself alone, and not in another."*

When it speaks of "rejoicing in himself alone, and not in another," it is talking about comparing yourself to others. We all struggle with the temptation of self-righteousness. "Well, I have done a lot of things, but I never would do that. How can he call himself a Christian and do that? I cannot believe it..." All of these are self-righteous statements we make when comparing ourselves to others.

It is amazing how we can understand our sin, but not another's. You do not know what a person has gone through. You do not know what is happening in their life at the present. You do not know what they have been taught. None of that should matter. We should simply have compassion for those who have fallen, regardless of how disgusting their sin may seem to us.

I have often dealt with situations where the church was up in arms about someone, only to find they did not have the facts. I remember one case where a man brutalized his wife. He verbally, sexually and physically abused her. She lived in constant fear. He was able to mask his behavior. In public he was "Mr. Spiritual" married to "Ms. Carnal." The way he forced her to live affected many areas of her life, which were easily visible. Because of her fear of him, she would say whatever he required. No one knew the truth. Here was someone who needed to be loved and encouraged, facing unbelievable circumstances, with no help from the church. Why? They looked at what they could see, passed judgement and determined not to help her, all the while providing love and acceptance for her abuser.

There is no room for judgement in any area of ministry, especially the restoration ministry. We only know what we can see from our perspective. Regardless of who is right or wrong, they still deserve help. Our job is to restore. Faults are simply the outward manifestation of needs. People must know that we will help them regardless of who is right.

Isaiah 42:1-3,7 describes certain aspects of Jesus ministry. *"Behold my servant, whom I uphold; mine elect, in whom my soul delighteth; I have put my spirit upon him: he shall bring forth judgment to the Gentiles. He shall not cry, nor lift up, nor cause his voice to be heard in the street. A bruised reed shall he not break, and the smoking flax shall he not quench: he shall bring forth judgment unto truth. To open the blind eyes, to bring out the prisoners from the prison,*

and them that sit in darkness out of the prison house."
Verse 7 tells of Jesus bringing the prisoners out of
prison. These are the people who have been destroyed
and marred because of their sin. They probably deserve to be where they are, but Jesus came to set the
captives free--whether they deserve it or not.

Verse 1 says Jesus will bring judgement to
them. That word "judgement" means "a verdict,
whether favorable or unfavorable." Since He is bringing them out of prison, the verdict is obviously favorable. Since Jesus carried all sin and all punishment for
sin, **every** man has a favorable verdict with the Lord.
Whether we deserve it or not, He has come to proclaim
liberty to the captives. Verse 2 says He will not cry out
in the streets. We know that Jesus ministered in the
streets. This verse does not make sense until we look
at verse 3. Jesus did not cry out in judgement against
the weak and wounded. His was not the voice of
public condemnation.

A bruised reed is a reed that has been damaged
beyond use, but is not completely broken. Smoldering
flax is a wick that is not giving off any light, so it only
fills the room with smoke. Jesus does not break the
useless reed or snuff out the reproachable wick. This is
the tendency of the church. When people become of
no value, we throw them away. The churches have
raped people of their talents and money, only to throw
them away when they became a liability.

Jesus had good news for the backslidden. He
came to proclaim the year of jubilee: the debt is paid,
you do not have to stay in prison. What a person's sin
is does not matter. Jesus died to set them free, and we
should lovingly and meekly proclaim their freedom.

Not only are they freed from the sin, they are freed from the penalty. It is essential that they understand, it is not God who is bringing the penalty for their actions. Jesus took the penalty, and God would never put on us what Jesus suffered for us. To do so would be a rejection of His finished work.

When we experience pain and difficulty because of our sin, it is a simple matter of sowing and reaping. There are grave consequences to sin. It is not God, however, that is dealing out those consequences. It is this expectation of judgement from God that keeps people separated from God, not their sin.

Jeremiah 2:19 says, *"Thine own wickedness shall correct thee, and thy backslidings shall reprove thee: know, therefore, and see that it is an evil thing and bitter, that thou hast forsaken the LORD thy God, and that my fear is not in thee, saith the Lord GOD of hosts."* Galatians 6:8 presents the same truth in New Testament terms, *"For he that soweth to his flesh shall of the flesh reap corruption; but he that soweth to the Spirit shall of the Spirit reap life everlasting."* But, Jeremiah 3:22 promises, *"Return, ye backsliding children, and I will heal your backslidings. Behold, we come unto thee; for thou art the LORD our God."* Hosea 14:4 echoes the promise to the backslidden, *"I will heal their backsliding, I will love them freely: for mine anger is turned away from him."* Isaiah 55:7 is my favorite scripture to the backslidden, *"Let the wicked forsake his way, and the unrighteous man his thoughts: and let him return unto the LORD, and he will have mercy upon him; and to our God, for he will abundantly pardon."* All of these scriptures depict God's desire to heal and restore the backslidden. Since this is God's view, we should have the same view.

Forgiveness with restoration is totally foreign to the natural mind. While I meet some that have a heart for forgiveness, I meet few that have a heart for restoration. We, like the elder brother in the parable of the prodigal son, tend to despise the goodness of the Lord in the area of restoration. We tend to say, "Forgive them Father, but make sure they suffer enough before you restore any of the benefits of sonship." Our views are so foreign to God's in this area that we are warned in Isaiah 55:8-9, *"For my thoughts are not your thoughts, neither are your ways my ways, saith the LORD. For as the heavens are higher than the earth, so are my ways higher than your ways, and my thoughts than your thoughts."* Do not think that the way you view the backslidden is the way God views them.

If our goal is truly repentance, then we must commit ourselves to the Lord's standard for restoration. God's method of bringing about repentance is goodness. *"Or despisest thou the riches of his goodness and forbearance and longsuffering; not knowing that the goodness of God leadeth thee to repentance?"* Romans 2:4. When this commitment is established in the church, we will no longer lose so many people to the world. Love and kindness not only restore the backslider, they keep him in relationship with God.

When I was backslidden, no one brought me a message of mercy. On the other hand, I heard plenty of judgement. Those I had helped over the years, the ones I had restored, turned their backs on me. Some of my preacher friends openly stated that I was too much of a liability. I was in sin; I needed help, but it seemed help was only offered if I would receive judgement.

Long after I had repented of my sin, I would hear people say, "I do not believe he has really repented." I used to wonder, "How would they know? They avoid me like the plague." I soon began to understand what people really meant, "I have not seen him suffer enough." The backslider is always suffering. Regardless of what he shows outwardly, he is always in pain.

The only way I could get restored was by getting away from Christians. When I was able to reduce the problem to God and me, it became very simple to solve. He gives me nothing but mercy, love and acceptance. It will take nothing less on my part to restore the fallen that I find along the wayside.

The struggling believer should never be forced to withdraw from the church. It is rare that a person in isolation will ever be recovered. Isolation becomes a breeding ground for all manner of delusion.

It is not our place to judge, fix, condemn or acquit. It is our job to provide an environment of love and mercy that facilitates restoration.

26

Essentials for New Believers

A proper foundation for faith must be established in the new believer if he is to grow and maintain stability. One of the fundamental reasons for an eventual failure in the Christian walk is a faulty foundation. Psalm 11:3 says, *"If the foundations be destroyed, what can the righteous do?"*

While attending Bible college, I saw many men and women fall. I was utterly amazed that a person could backslide in Bible College, yet it seemed to be happening all around me. Of the people I talked to, the vast majority had a desire to live for the Lord, but there always seemed to be some "mystical force" hindering them.

I could never be satisfied with the general answers given by those in trouble. As I questioned them, I soon found they did not understand the problem. After extensive probing, I found the problem to be "foundational." They were ignorant of some of the foundational truths of the gospel, *"My people are destroyed for lack of knowledge..."* Hosea 4:6.

Knowledge is essential for walking by faith. We cannot operate faith for that which we do not know. "*...Through knowledge shall the just be deliv-ered.*" Proverbs 11:9. Discouragement and confusion plague the believer who does not have a stable foundation.

In recent years, there has been a wonderful increase in the teaching ministry. This restoration of the teaching ministry has brought wonderful truth to the Body of Christ. However, one of the strengths of the teaching revival has also been one of its greatest weaknesses.

In a church that is strong in Bible teaching, there is a tendency to forget the basics. Along with every real move of God, there is an equivalent danger. With every truth there is a new opportunity for misunderstanding, and with every movement there is an occasion for abuse. The teaching ministry, which I am in no way criticizing, has a way of creating an environment that thrives on "new or deep" knowledge. This is an age old problem. "*For the Jews require a sign, and the Greeks seek after wisdom.*" 1 Corinthians 1:22.

In an attempt to meet the legitimate need for more knowledge and insight, we often overlook the basics. This is what I call building "skyscrapers on mud puddles." To load a new believer with deep spiritual truth, independent of a solid foundation, will guarantee collapse. Therefore, it is essential that we teach every new convert certain basics.

Our first step is through our Sponsor's Program. In this program, another believer is assigned to the new convert for six weeks. Each week the new convert is taught the very basic steps in following the Lord. Another great tool is a new believer's foundation class. For a church that is reaching new people, it is essential to have such a class as an ongoing part of the program. Every new church member, and especially the new convert, should attend this class.

The first subject that must be taught is "Faith toward God and Repentance from Dead Works." This is the place where assurance of salvation is made clear apart from works. In this class, a new believer will become confident in his salvation. Once salvation by faith is clear, it is nearly impossible to undermine the new believer's confidence.

In learning repentance from dead works, one is introduced to the grace of God. Traditionally, grace has been defined as unmerited favor. However, grace is more accurately defined as the power or ability of God that works in us, to make us able, to live the Christian life.[1] The writer of Hebrews says, *"Be not carried about with divers and strange doctrines. For it is a good thing that the heart be established with grace..."* Hebrews 13:9. One must quickly learn to depend on and draw from the grace of God.

In this same class one must be introduced to the Lordship of Jesus. While a commitment to Lordship is made at the new birth, it must be understood completely. Because many people have been introduced to Jesus as Savior and not Lord, they never live in consistent victory.

The Lordship of Jesus is expressed through the written Word. One is only committed to the LORD-SHIP of Jesus to the degree he is committed to the

---

[1] The *"Grace: The Power to Change"* James B. Richards, Impact International Publications, Huntsville, Alabama

written Word. We must immediately take believers from the realm of choice and preference to the realm of Lordship; when you find it in the Word, believe it and do it in faith.

One major hurdle that must be crossed is renewing the mind. After an absolute commitment to Lordship is established, transforming the thought life must follow. Just as we get ability to act differently, we can get ability (grace) to win over our thoughts.

Whatever a person allows to live in their thoughts will ultimately be fulfilled in their actions. With our complex, perverted society, most people are tormented with all kinds of evil thoughts. If they do not win this battle, they will not win other battles. If they are tormented through an out-of-control thought life, sin will still rule a major portion of their life.

Before moving on to the other major Biblical truths, the last hurdle is identity, self-image and self-worth. Everything about our society destroys our God-given sense of self-worth. I believe self-worth to be the deepest need in mankind. It is at the root of all our life-dominating actions. We have become new creatures; we must see ourselves as God now sees us.

Self-centeredness is at the root of every sin. Self-worth is the determining factor in the conflict between self-centeredness and sacrifice. In John 13, we have the account of Jesus washing the disciples' feet. *"Now before the feast of the Passover, when Jesus knew that his hour was come that he should depart out of this world unto the Father, having loved his own which were in the world, he loved them unto the end. And supper being ended, the devil having now put into the heart of Judas Iscariot, Simon's son, to betray him;*

Jesus knowing that the Father had given all things into his hands, and that he was come from God, and went to God; He riseth from supper, and laid aside his garments; and took a towel, and girded himself. After that he poureth water into a basin, and began to wash the disciples' feet, and to wipe them with the towel wherewith he was girded." John 13:1-5.

Jesus' ability to humble himself was based on verse 3, *"...Knowing that...He was come from God and went to God."* Knowing who He was kept Him free from the need to make a name for Himself. He was free from self-centeredness because He was free from performance-based self-worth. He found total fulfillment in His relationship with the Father. Thus, He was free to obey.

Obedience is never difficult for the one whose identity and self-worth is found through a personal relationship with the Lord Jesus. If there is a faulty sense of self-worth, disobedience will vary according to the way the situation affects our sense of self-worth.

We, like Jesus, must lose ourselves in our relationship and our purpose in God. *"Jesus saith unto them, My meat is to do the will of him that sent me, and to finish his work."* John 4:34. *"And he said unto them, How is it that ye sought me? wist ye not that I must be about my Father's business?"* Luke 2:49 *"I can of mine own self do nothing: as I hear, I judge: and my judgment is just; because I [seek not mine own] will, but the will of the Father which hath sent me."* John 5:30. *"And I seek not mine own glory: there is one that seeketh and judgeth."* John 8:50.

One essential that is often overlooked by many independent churches is water baptism. Water baptism is more than obedience or ritual. Water baptism is the place where one can put works with his faith for newness of life. Baptism in and of itself, does nothing for the new believer. However, when it is done in faith it can make all the difference in the world. Romans 6:3-4 says, *"Know ye not, that so many of us as were baptized into Jesus Christ were baptized into his death? Therefore we are buried with him by baptism into death: that like as Christ was raised up from the dead by the glory of the Father, even so we also should walk in newness of life."*

Baptism does not save the individual. Baptism is not to identify with the resurrection; it is to identify with the death of the Lord. Baptism is the place where one, by faith, identifies with the death of Jesus and the death of his old nature. When this is done in faith, the grace of God comes forth to give the ability to die to the past.

However, baptism does not stop at death; it is only complete by a resurrection into newness of life. Just as we believe we lay the old man down in death with Christ, we should also believe we are raised up in His power as a new creation, able to live in newness of life. *"In whom also ye are circumcised with the circumcision made without hands, in putting off the body of the sins of the flesh by the circumcision of Christ: Buried with him in baptism, wherein also ye are risen with him through the faith of the operation of God, who hath raised him from the dead."* Colossians 2:11-12.

Because the new believer is never taught to operate faith for the death of the old man and resurrection of the new man, grace never comes to make it an experiential reality. Therefore, the Christian walk often turns to legalism and works. Stress and frustration then dominate life. With faith in newness of life through the Lord Jesus, there is grace in our hearts to serve God and overcome the past. Life is easy and light.

With this as a solid foundation, we can build our lives as spiritual skyscrapers that glorify God. They will endure the storms and the attacks of the enemy. *"Therefore whosoever heareth these sayings of mine, and doeth them, I will liken him unto a wise man, which built his house upon a rock: And the rain descended, and the floods came, and the winds blew, and beat upon that house; and it fell not: for it was rounded upon a rock."* Matthew 7:24-25. Build on a solid foundation, experience a continual flow of God's grace and you will never fail.[2]

---

[2] The *"Foundations of Faith Workbook"* is available through Impact International Publications, 3300 North Broad Place, Huntsville, Alabama 35805.

27

Evangelism and Spiritual Warfare

One of the greatest misunderstandings in twentieth-century Christianity is spiritual warfare. Our concept of spiritual warfare is huddling together in a building or arena and screaming at the devils until they give up their position of power and preeminence in a city.

While we should pray, much of this has become little more than "spiritual" activity that produces almost no favorable results. We should do spiritual warfare, but we must do it the Bible way if we are to achieve Bible results.

In Acts 4, the church began to experience persecution from the governmental/religious leaders. They had already seen Jesus crucified, so they knew what the leaders had the potential to do to them. When Peter and John were arrested for working a miracle, the church gathered to pray. Verse 24 is a key verse. *"...They lifted up their voice to God with one accord..."* It says two significant things: First, they lifted up their voice to God, not the devil. In the spiritual warfare of our day, all the attention is focused on the devil. If Jesus defeated the devil, we need not spend all night screaming at him. God must be the focus of our prayers, not the devil.

It is not enough to bind the wrong thing, you have got to loose the right thing. It seems we have lost sight of the fact that binding is only half of our operation of authority. Matthew 16:19, *"And I will give unto thee the keys of the kingdom of heaven: and whatsoever thou shalt bind on earth shall be bound in heaven: and whatsoever thou shalt loose on earth shall be loosed in heaven."* The early church was not devil-oriented, but God oriented. They exercised their authority over the devil when necessary and then went about doing the works of God.

Second, they were all of one accord. They were in total agreement about what must be done. The following verses show that their "warfare" was for the purpose of obtaining boldness to go forth and witness. *"And now, Lord, behold their threatenings: and grant unto thy servants, that with all boldness they may speak thy word, By stretching forth thine hand to heal; and that signs and wonders may be done by the name of thy holy child Jesus."* Acts 4:29-30.

They did not hide in the church, scream at the devil, and expect to cast him out of the sky. They gathered in the church, prayed to God, and went forth casting the devil out of people. Their prayer was for boldness so they could go forth and do the work. Since they prayed in faith, believing God heard them, they went forth and acted on their faith. The results were phenomenal. *"And with great power gave the apostles witness of the resurrection of the Lord Jesus: and great grace was upon them all. And by the hands of the apostles were many signs and wonders wrought among the people; (and they were all with one accord in Solomon's porch...) Insomuch that they brought forth the sick into the streets, and laid them on beds and couches, that at the least the shadow of Peter passing by might overshadow some of them. There came also a multitude out of the cities round about unto Jerusalem, bringing sick folks, and them which were vexed with unclean spirits: and they were healed every one."* Acts 4:33, 5:12,15,16. Because they put their attention on God, they received grace (God's ability) to go forth and do real spiritual warfare.

Likewise, the growth they enjoyed came as a result of their ministry. *"And believers were the more added to the Lord, multitudes both of men and women."* Acts 5:14. While prayer is the essential prerequisite for ministry, it can never become the substitute. Beating up the devil cannot be a substitute for glorifying God.

Ephesians 6:12 has become the cornerstone verse for doing spiritual warfare over a city.[1] *"For we wrestle not against flesh and blood, but against principalities, against powers, against the rulers of the darkness of this world, against spiritual wickedness in high places."* This verse presents a concept of a hierarchy in the demonic realm. Additionally, there is no doubt that specific kinds of spirits affect our cities. Without question, we should exercise our authority to conquer these spirits.

However, we must never forget that demonic

[1] For a thorough knowledge of our victory over Satan one should read *"Satan Unmasked."* James B. Richards, Impact International Publications, Huntsville, Alabama

spirits work through people, not in the air. If demons have no one to cooperate with them, they cannot function. The regimentation of demons is clearly seen in the Old Testament. Many times the Bible will speak of a certain prince or country; then proceeds to make reference to a demonic prince with the same name. It is more than obvious that the demonic princes worked through the leaders of those countries. So much so that they were called by the same name: the prince of Tyre, the prince of Grecia, the prince of Persia.

In Daniel 10, Daniel prayed for specific revelation knowledge. The messenger, Gabriel was sent with the needed information. The prince of Persia, however, detained Gabriel for 21 days. *"Then said he unto me, Fear not, Daniel: for from the first day that thou didst set thine heart to understand, and to chasten thyself before thy God, thy words were heard, and I am come for thy words. But, the prince of the kingdom of Persia withstood me one and twenty days: but, lo, Michael, one of the chief princes, came to help me, and I remained there with the kings of Persia."* Daniel 10:12-13. This prince of Persia was obviously a demonic principality. Yet, his influence on earth came through the leader of Persia.

Later in the chapter, Gabriel spoke of the prince of Grecia who was to come. *"Then said he, Knowest thou wherefore I come unto thee? And now will I return to fight with the prince of Persia: and when I am gone forth, the prince of Grecia shall come."* Daniel 10:20. The angel is obviously speaking of the demonic prince who influenced that country. But it must be known that those demons ruled through the leaders of the country. Demons must have people through which they work.

The only way to capture a city or a country is to win its leaders. If you can win those leaders to Jesus, they will no longer yield to unrighteousness. Or if you can win the people, they will not follow unrighteous leaders and you can stop demonic rule. But, you can scream at the devil all day long and never change a city.

Unrighteous people will rule in unrighteousness. We must win the lost and turn them to righteousness. Otherwise change will never come. America was built on godly principles. There is absolutely no doubt about the intentions of our founding fathers. Because the church has failed to evangelize our nation, we have had unrighteous men twist our constitution to the point it is being used to prevent religious freedom. No amount of laws passed will ever stop the unrighteous from being unrighteous. No amount of binding and loosing the devil, without evangelism and ministry, will ever stop the flood of unrighteousness.

The following scriptures reveal the need for righteousness in government. Proverbs 14:34 says, *"Righteousness exalteth a nation: but sin is a reproach to any people."* Proverbs 25:5, *"Take away the wicked from before the king, and his throne shall be established in righteousness."* Proverbs 28:28 says, *"When the wicked rise, men hide themselves: but when they perish, the righteous increase."* Proverbs 29:2 says *"When the righteous are in authority, the people rejoice: but when the wicked beareth rule, the people mourn."* Proverbs 29:16 says, *"When the wicked are multiplied, transgression increaseth: but the righteous shall see their fall."* We must pray over a city, and we must intercede. But until people believe on the Lord Jesus Christ, righteousness will not come and men will not change. Romans 10:10 says, *"For with the heart man BELIEVETH UNTO RIGHTEOUSNESS..."*

When Paul went to Athens and found them totally given to idolatry, he did not bind the devil in the air. He bound the devil in people by preaching to them. *"Now while Paul waited for them at Athens, his spirit was stirred in him, when he saw the city wholly given to idolatry. Therefore, disputed he in the synagogue with the Jews, and with the devout persons, and in the market daily with them that met with him."* Acts 17:16-17.

The two most legitimate types of spiritual warfare are: (1) when we conquer the sin in our own lives so we can live for Jesus and (2) when we conquer sin in others and lead them to victory in Jesus. Anything else is venturing into the realm of fantasy, not ministry.

A few years ago, I had the good opportunity to meet Omar Cabrerro from Argentina. He is a very kind and genuine man. I heard him teach about spiritual warfare. I talked with him about the evangelism that follows the prayer meetings. You see, after they pray over a city they go in and take it by evangelism. They have won hundreds of thousands of people to the Lord.

I have read and heard of Americans that visit his country. Having visited, they assume to be experts on the subject and come to America to teach on spiritual warfare. I am always amazed at the way evangelism is left out or de-emphasized.

The same thing happens when Americans hear Dr. Cho of Korea. They come home, start early morning prayer, all night prayer meetings and cell groups, but somehow they miss the whole purpose of all these activities...TO WIN THE LOST!

Apart from coupling evangelism with all of our prayer and programs, it is little more than "spiritual entertainment." While we play "spiritual games," multitudes are entering eternity without Jesus. While we are "warring for our city," the sin rules through the hearts of corrupt people. Do not stop praying. Do not stop early morning prayer. Do not stop anything; just start doing it for the right reason. After you pray...minister to the people.

Much of the frustration in the church today is the result of putting forth so much time and effort and seeing so little results. Yet, in churches who train the people to minister, there is an amazing excitement. Jesus conquered the devil. Instead of us attempting to fight that same battle again, let's proclaim to the world that they are free from his power.

28

The Plan of Action

Now you have your plan. All you have to do is implement it. If this becomes another book you simply read and fail to implement, we have both wasted our time. Develop a lifestyle that will create and be sensitive to opportunities to serve others through personal ministry.

It will always be convenient to ignore the hurts and sorrows of people around you. Fear will often compel you to ignore their needs; yet, the heart of ministry is serving. There will be questions you cannot answer. There will be needs that you cannot meet. But, you can always pray and encourage.

Once while conducting a seminar in a local church, I held day classes on evangelism. The pastor attended these classes like everyone else. He was very enthused about the people who went out witnessing and won the lost.

One afternoon we went to work out at a local gym. While swimming in the pool, we began to talk to a man about the Lord. The pastor did a great job at initiating the conversation; but when he began to witness to him, he lost it. He did not apply what he had learned that week.

After several minutes, I asked if I could say something. I shared "Creation to Calvary" and in three minutes we were praying the sinner's prayer. (We baptized the man in the swimming pool with everyone watching. It was great!) Trust this method. Put it into practice, and you will see results.

Once, while having a well-known evangelist visit my home, I received a phone call. The lady on the other end wanted to send someone over to receive ministry. I thought I would allow the evangelist the honor of ministering salvation to the young man after he arrived.

The evangelist shared his testimony; the man traveling with him shared his testimony; it was unbelievable. After more than thirty minutes I interrupted, "Could I say something please?" I shared "Creation to Calvary," and in three to five minutes we were praying the sinners prayer.

I am always open to anything the Lord wants to do. I know the need to be spontaneous and creative, but when it gets down to salvation I am going to work the plan.

Late one night, while recovering from surgery, I was awakened by a nurse who said, "I saw on your chart that you were a minister." "Yes," I sleepily replied. "We have a lady dying. Could you please help? She has been screaming for days." The request came. Because of the tubes in my stomach, we had to "rig up" an apparatus for carrying my bottles and tubes, but finally we got underway to the lady's room. As we rolled down the hall, I could hear her screams of fear and pain. The room had the stench of death. There in the bed lay Rosie, a large, black woman who had several different diseases.

Rosie was a member of a little Methodist church. I had met a member of her church who was not saved. I met her pastor, and he was not saved. So I doubted seriously whether she actually knew the Lord. But I knew I could not just come in and challenge her salvation. I was there to win her to Jesus, not win an argument.

After a brief introduction and a short prayer, Rosie calmed down enough to talk. As we talked, I listened for my opportunity. When she began telling me what all she had done for the church, I knew her faith was in the wrong place.

I said, "Rosie, have you ever seen a vision?" "Naw sir," she answered. "Well, tonight you are going to see a vision from the Lord; just close your eyes," I instructed. "Now Rosie, I want you to see yourself young, slender and healthy. You are about sixteen years old, and you are walking up a hill. The hill is covered with beautiful green grass. There's a gentle breeze blowing as you walk up the hill. Then you hear it - the most beautiful music you have ever heard. As you top the hill you see it; it is the city of God, New Jerusalem. Oh it is so beautiful." "Yessir, I see it, I see it," she said, "it's beautiful."

"Look Rosie, Jesus is coming out to meet you. Do you see Him?" I asked. "Oh yessir I sho do," she said. "He has a question for you Rosie, He wants to know why He should let you in heaven," I said. Rosie began to talk to Jesus Himself. She began to list her works, "I always went to church, all the time," she explained. I whispered, "That is not the answer." "I always sang in the choir, every Sunday," her expectancy heightened. "No, that is not the answer either," I said. She went on to explain all her good deeds.

Finally, I said, "Rosie, none of your good works will get you into heaven." I explained "Creation to Calvary." Immediately she cried out, "Jesus, I trust you. You paid the price for my sin. You were raised from the dead. You are my Lord, I trust you Jesus."

Relief came for Rosie that night. Such joy came into her she began to sing. She sang in the way only the old black churches can do. "Lord, bless the white boy, ahhh. He done told me about Jesus, ahhh. He done showed me the way of salvation, ahhh. He done showed me a vision, ahhh. He done showed me a vision 'bout Jesus. He done showed me the way of salvation." The screams that had previously filled the halls were now replaced with songs of praise and thanksgiving.

Just a short time later, Rosie went home to be with Jesus. I am so thankful for Holy Ghost creativity, but I am also thankful that I have a plan. When it is time to get down to business, I have a plan. I am always open for the leading of the Lord, and I would do anything I felt Him lead in. But I have never yet had to deviate far from "Creation to Calvary." There may be times I give a shorter or longer version, but I always use this plan.

Once, while driving down the highway, I saw a young black man walking down an intersecting road. My heart was touched when I saw him, so I began to pray for him. The Holy Spirit spoke to my heart and said, "You know that is not what I want you to do." So I turned around and went back.

When I pulled alongside of him and stopped my car, he looked a little frightened. I quickly explained, "I was driving down the highway and saw you walking and the Lord spoke to my heart about you." As I spoke, a word of knowledge came to me, I said, "You are in despair and about to give up, you do not know which way to turn or where to go; but God has not forsaken you." He was amazed. He explained how he had just lost his job; his wife had left, and he did not know what to do.

I invited this young man to sit in my car as I explained "Creation to Calvary." With tears rolling down his face, he prayed and made Jesus Lord. After we talked for a few minutes he explained, "My father is a Baptist minister, but I have never in my life heard the Gospel the way you explained it. For the first time, I understand what Jesus did for me."

Many people are afraid of committing to a particular plan for fear of actually having to do something. Preachers have been the most reluctant to follow a plan. Many people are so outgoing and creative they can "fly by their pants," but most people are not that way. Unfortunately, many disqualify themselves from personal ministry for a lack of creativity and persuasiveness.

All our methods must be transferable. If I can transfer a method to another person and give him room to put in his personality, I have multiplied my ministry and experience. Therefore, when people see me do it the same every time, they realize that it is not my power or persuasiveness that gets the job done. Those who improvise every time can never teach anyone what they do.

Several times preachers have come to me for help. When I teach them, they get a little stiff-necked. They start telling me how they know what they are doing. They do not need to commit to a particular plan. (I always wonder why they come to me if what they have is working so well.) But I simply look them in the eye and ask, "How many people have you led to Jesus this year?" I usually get a real spiritual answer like, "A whole lot." I simply ask, "How many?" After a lengthy game of "nail down the preacher," I get the truth-very few, if any.

I simply explain, "Once you have used some-one else's plan and won several hundred people to the Lord, you have earned the right to experiment. But you have no right trying anything of your own until you have success. Lives are too precious to waste on our religious experiments." Some will ask, "Did you work someone else's plan before you developed you own?" I sure did. I won dozens, if not hundreds to the Lord using what we called the "Roman's Road to Salvation," but experience showed me the limitations and some of the unscriptural concepts to this method. As I became seasoned as a soul winner, I developed a plan that was scriptural and workable.

"Creation to Calvary" is the basic outline for all personal and public ministry. Every need of hu-manity was met through Jesus' work of death, burial and resurrection. It is what a person believes about these events that empowers him in every area of life.

I could go on and on about creative opportuni-ties that I followed the Lord into, but you need your own experiences. Go out and do it! If you do not have the courage to start alone, come to Huntsville and go out with one of our teams. Order the accompanying tape set with the same title as this book. Do all that you can do to prepare; but whatever you do, do **something.** Do not sit around doing nothing.

There are people that no one other than you can help. Your circle of influence needs you to influence them for Jesus. Give them the Word in love. Even if they turn you off now, they will come to you later when they are ready for help.

Unleash the power of God that came into you the day you got saved. Go out and MAKE AN IMPACT FOR JESUS!

The person who decides to live a life of love for others enters a never-ending adventure. Every situation becomes an experience of the life of God that flows out of them.

BIBLIOGRAPHY

Cho, Paul Y. *More Than Numbers.* Waco: Word Books, 1984

Kennedy, James D. *Evangelism Explosion.* Wheaton: Tyndale House, 1973

Lea, Larry. *Mending Broken Nets & Broken Fishermen.* Rockwall: Church on the Rock, 1986

Osborn, T.L. *Soul Winning.* Tulsa: Harrison House, 1980

Richards, James B. *The Gospel of Peace.* Huntsville: Impact International Publications, 1990

Richards, James B. *Satan Unmasked.* Huntsville: Impact International Publications, 1998

Richards, James B. *My Church, My Family: How to Have a Healthy Relationship with the Church.* Huntsville: Impact International Publications, 1995

Richards, James B. *Sponsor's Workbook.* Huntsville: Impact International Publications, 1998

Richards, James B. *Foundations of Faith Workbook.* Huntsville: Impact International Publications, 1998

Richards, James B. *Relevant Ministry Workbook.* Huntsville: Impact International Publications, 1998

Savelle, Jerry. *Sharing Jesus Effectively.* Tulsa: Harrison House, 1982

Strong, James. *Strong's Exhaustive Concordance.* Grand Rapids: Baker, 1972

Thayer, Joseph H. trans. *A Greek-English Lexicon of the New Testament.* Grand Rapids: Baker, 1977

Vaughn, Curtis, ed., *The Bible from 26 Translations.* Grand Rapids: Baker, 1988

Wagner, C. Peter, *Your Church Can Grow.* Ventura: Regal Books, 1976

The Expositor's Bible Commentary, Zondervan Publishing Company, Grand Rapids, Michigan

The New International Bible, Zondervan Publishing Company, Grand Rapids, Michigan

All scriptures are quoted from The King James Version of the Bible unless otherwise indicated.